IN FOCUS

TAROT

Your Personal Guide

STEVEN BRIGHT

WELLFLEET
PRESS

Inspiring | Educating | Creating | Entertaining

Brimming with creative inspiration, how-to projects, and useful
information to enrich your everyday life, Quarto Knows is a favorite
destination for those pursuing their interests and passions. Visit our
site and dig deeper with our books into your area of interest:
Quarto Creates, Quarto Cooks, Quarto Homes, Quarto Lives,
Quarto Drives, Quarto Explores, Quarto Gifts, or Quarto Kids.

First published in 2018 by Wellfleet Press,
an imprint of The Quarto Group
142 West 36th Street, 4th Floor
New York, NY 10018 USA
T (212) 779-4972 F (212) 779-6058
www.QuartoKnows.com

10 9 8 7 6 5

ISBN: 978-1-57715-208-8

Cover and Interior Design: Ashley Prine, Tandem Books

Printed in China

CONTENTS

1

GETTING STARTED

What Is Tarot?

The tarot that we recognize today is a set of seventy-eight illustrated cards. Whether you have used tarot before or not, you're probably aware of a few of its main players. Most people will call to mind the enigmatic Death card whenever the tarot is mentioned. If not Death, then it might be The Lovers, since both cards have been used many times in fiction and popular culture. There are, however, seventy-six additional cards, probably less recognizable, that make up a standard tarot pack. You might be surprised to know that Death and The Lovers are less frequent visitors to a reader's table than they appear in the pages of novels or in television dramas!

Tarot has a shady history, and for that reason, we will not look into it too deeply here. There have been many conflicting theories as to how and when it originated, but most modern tarot commentators settle on Renaissance Italy as being the time and place that tarot made its public debut. The oldest and most complete deck in existence is the Visconti-Sforza, dating back to the fifteenth century, the cards of which now rest in museums and with collectors around the world.

What is known about tarot is that it has ducked in and out of fashion throughout history, being damned by the church in the second half of the fourteenth century, resurrected by the occultists in the late nineteenth century, and adopted by the New Age community not long after. Tarot's traditional meanings have evolved, as has its style and use. These days, tarot cards are used for far more than they ever were previously, and they provide counsel and comfort for people the world over. Tarot's use as an aid for reflection, healing, and psychological analysis is popular, as is its use within magical work and for fortune telling.

Tarot can help us unlock our deepest feelings, confront our fears, and successfully guide us through the darker aspects of life. Whether used for daily affirmations or to gauge the next best step, most would agree that the real power of the tarot is not within the cards themselves—since they are no more than paper and ink—but within the intention of the users and how they interpret these symbols for the best good. Tarot must not rob us of our personal power and capabilities but, instead, should empower and help us to live a richer life. The cards can do this by showing readers how to tap in to potential opportunities, providing them with ways we can effectively swerve around or confront the obstacles on our path.

What Tarot Is Not

While tarot can help us to decipher problems and unlock obstacles, it is most effectively used when concentrating on the present time. While it can locate issues that have played an important part in our past or that will have a significant bearing on the future, it is worth remembering that our future is not set in stone. The tarot cards are best used as a tool to help provoke changes, rather than seal our future with uncompromising fate. Not everyone realizes this when they receive a reading. A common misconception of tarot is that it predicts an unyielding future that we have no control over.

While the cards will accurately pinpoint relevant situations, they are not a replacement for medical advice. When in a state of ill health, many will consult a reader, hoping that they'll receive the "all clear" in the cards. Although the tarot can often detect when something is wrong, it cannot advise a solution for a medical problem. While this might seem obvious, you'd be surprised how many seek answers around health in a tarot reading. Someone seeking medical guidance should speak to a doctor before consulting a tarot reader. The tarot may help you deal with a health-related problem emotionally, but it cannot diagnose what is wrong or suggest the best treatment.

Many people believe that tarot is part of the practice of witchcraft or is a replacement for religion. These are also false beliefs. While many practicing witches use tarot, it is not synonymous with either witchcraft or Wicca. Tarot is used by people of all religions and by those with no religious affinity. For most, it is a tool to help them enhance their spiritual beliefs, rather than acting as a replacement for it.

Is Tarot Dangerous?

It is important to acknowledge, right at the beginning of this book, that tarot is not dangerous. This is something that some believe, but it is far from the truth. Religion and popular media have instilled fear within the minds and hearts of many, muddying the good work and reputation of many skilled readers.

Think for a second, if you would, of the humble knife. Most of us pick one up every day, whether to butter our bread or to cut food. However, you'd probably not be surprised to hear that the most common knives used in assaults are ones taken from the kitchen. Should we brand all knives as murder weapons? Of course we shouldn't. A knife is only a weapon if determined so by the person using it.

It would be fair to say that not everyone uses the tarot cards with positive intention. While the cards may have less potential to physically harm than a knife, some are fearful of the tarot and think that using it could be dangerous. As with the example of the kitchen knife, this can only be determined by the user. There will always be people who choose to use their tools to appear powerful or as a way of controlling others. But when used with sensitivity, compassion, and responsibility, the wealth of the tarot images and their meanings can be sought to find peace and direction. As we will discover, the seemingly darker images within the seventy-eight-card deck—like those of Death and The Devil—are simply reflections of our own motivations and aspects of our life journey. In many cases, these symbols needn't be feared but embraced. Life is not entirely positive or entirely negative. The tarot deck reflects this and seeks to establish a sense of balance.

Some tarot designers have sought to provide decks with overtly positive depictions on the cards. It would be true to say that no card in the tarot deck is entirely light or entirely dark, but sweeping anything that is seemingly worrying under the spiritual carpet is not a reflection of the human experience. We all face difficulties and obstacles. It is a fact of life. It is the way in which we respond to these events that is important. Do we confront them, or do we try to hide from them?

Who Can Use Tarot?

The short answer to this is: anyone. Contrary to common belief, you do not need to have psychic skills to read the cards, nor need you be part of a certain group, or hold a specific set of spiritual beliefs. If we have a positive intention and an open mind, the tarot cards are an effective tool for delving deeper into our intuition and unconscious motivations. Working like a mirror, the cards reflect not only what is happening, but also those things of which we might not be consciously aware at the present time.

How Can You Get the Most Out of This Book?

We all learn differently, so how you gain the most from this book will be individual to you. That said, the book has been set up with both the beginner and intermediate reader in mind. For the tarot newcomer, it can be read from cover to cover, but it is likely that most tarot students will wish to use it as a resource that they can dip in and out of. Within chapters two and three, each card from the tarot deck is explained on five different levels:

Introduction

To begin, the card is introduced with its general meaning. This section describes the flavor of the card and how it is traditionally viewed.

The Card as a Situation

One of the hardest things for a reader to do is translate the antique ideas of the tarot deck into the modern age. This section suggests ways in which each card could be viewed within a current, everyday situation.

The Card as a Person

Learning to be flexible with card meanings can be difficult. In this section, I describe how each tarot card might describe a person. There will be times when a card is used as a significator (more about that on page 189) or to describe someone in your life. Understanding how the card can be perceived in this way shows how each card can be determined in a multitude of different tarot spreads or positions.

The Card and You

Even though we might have learned the essence of a card's meaning, it doesn't stop us from experiencing blocks from time to time. This section lists prompts that can help kick-start your intuition or help you relate to a card's message on a personal level.

Keywords

The keywords are a source of quick and handy meanings. I have included those that I feel help to provide a well-rounded interpretation of each card. If you want to refresh your memory quickly, you can read just the keywords.

The Universal Waite Tarot

The New Age era of the 1970s ushered in a massive interest in the tarot, and those who wanted to use these mysterious cards started to look around for suitable decks. There were very few in existence at that time, and while most had some kind of illustrations on the Major Arcana, the Minor Arcana cards looked no better than playing cards.

Right from the start, however, one deck stood out: the Rider-Waite Tarot. This deck contained clear illustrations of each of the seventy-eight cards, and so it became the deck of choice for many tarot readers. The only downside was that the colors were considered somewhat garish, so eventually, the Universal Waite Tarot came into being. This is an adaptation of Rider-Waite with slightly softer colors than the original that is still a very popular deck among both amateur and professional tarot readers.

Getting Familiar with Tarot

Choosing your tarot deck should be an enjoyable and magical experience. I can still remember how excited I felt when I bought my second set, the Röhrig Tarot, many moons ago. Back in those days, stores would display an album of samples, showing two or three cards from each of the decks that they could order. I was mesmerized, flipping through the album of images and eventually choosing the set to which I felt most connected.

These days, there are far more tarots on the market than when I started twenty years ago. They literally come in all shapes and sizes, in different themes, and on occasion, with different structures. While picking a tarot that you are drawn to is an important consideration, it does pay to ask a few questions or do a little research beforehand. I learned the hard way that not every deck has the same setup or core meanings.

A good New Age shop will be able to answer your questions, and with the internet at our fingertips, you'll find many reviewers and experts online who are happy to lend a helping hand.

At the end of the day, it really is important that you find a set of images that speaks to you. Using a deck of cards that you do not like will not assist your learning, and working with it could become a chore.

Making the Tarot Your Own

Within the tarot deck, you will find many different characters. You'll likely come up against a figure hanging upside down, a mystical priestess, several winged beings, and even the Grim Reaper himself. While many of these archetypes will seem obvious in meaning, there will be some that are more difficult for the modern reader to relate to than others. For example, what can a medieval chariot tell you about your life today?

Now that we are all immersed within modern technology, the concepts within the tarot cards may at first seem a little outdated; however, this could not be further from the truth. The age-old ideas and experiences displayed within the tarot card archetypes are potentially more important now than ever before, fulfilling the modern need for balance and reflection.

In this book, I have endeavored to bridge the gap between the antique imagery within the tarot cards and your personal day-to-day situations. How can a common fool spice up your love life or an elderly man with a lamp take you on a much-needed journey of self-discovery? I'm a great believer that the trick to understanding the tarot images is in using the cards as a reflection. When we look at an image and its generally accepted meanings, we can allow for it to mirror our own life situations—from our past, to our present, to even our potential future. Layering a card with your own experiences will help you to understand each of the tarot cards on a far deeper level.

How Is a Tarot Deck Structured?

It is generally accepted that a traditional tarot deck has seventy-eight cards. When you are shopping for your own set, there is a chance you'll find decks that come with either more or less. While there is the odd exception to every rule, most of these are not traditional tarot decks (*even* if it says so on the box). This is why it pays to do a little research beforehand. A badly researched deck can result in a lot of confusion and difficulty in the long run.

Within the seventy-eight cards, the tarot deck is broken down into two sections: the Major Arcana and the Minor Arcana. The word *arcana* (from Latin *arcanus*) translates as "secrets" or "mysteries." Therefore, the Major Arcana, comprising twenty-two cards, represents major shifts within our life path, and the Minor Arcana is connected to the mundane and "everyday" situations we might face.

Fire   Water   Air   Earth

The Minor Arcana is divided into four suits. The names of the suits will vary from deck to deck but the most widely used are those of Wands (also sometimes called Rods or Batons), Cups (or Chalices), Swords (or Knives), and Pentacles (or Coins or Stones). Each has an elemental association. Deck designers and illustrators assign these elements according to their own beliefs but the most widely recognized is Fire, Water, Air, and Earth, respectively.

Each of the four suits contains fourteen cards. The first ten cards are sometimes referred to as *Pips*. The final four cards of each suit are known as Court cards.

Examples of Major Arcana Cards

The Courts signify different personality types within a reading. Many tarot designers have changed the names they've given to the "people cards" in their decks, in accordance with the deck's theme, but the most popular titling is Page (followed by Daughter, Knave, or Princess), Knight (then Son, Cavalier, or Prince), Queen (or Mother), and King (or Father).

The tarot system described in this book stems from the Rider-Waite tradition and appears as follows:

- **The Major Arcana:** 22 cards
- **The Minor Arcana:** 56 cards, comprising 4 suits of 14 cards

The cards in the Major Arcana relate to the corresponding number cards in each of the Minor Arcana suits, especially cards 1 through 10. For example, a 9 card in any of the suits relates in some way to the Major Arcana's ninth card, The Hermit.

Examples of Minor Arcana Cards

The Meanings of the Suits

Each suit within the Minor Arcana has its own significance. While the cards from each will provide information in all manner of readings, their elements describe the suit's general characteristics.

The suit of Wands is connected to Fire. This element refers to our drive and enthusiasm. It is what motivates us to get things moving. In a reading, a succession of cards from this suit can determine an exciting situation or a boost of creativity.

The suit of Cups is connected to Water. The element of Water concerns our emotional life. It can often describe how we feel about something. Many cards from this suit in a reading can highlight romance or important personal relationships.

The suit of Swords is connected to Air. Air is associated with thoughts and communication. In a reading, many cards from this suit can suggest a need to approach things logically. In some cases, a string of cards from the suit of Swords can be problematic in a reading.

The suit of Pentacles is connected to Earth. This element is grounded and concerns our material life. If many cards from this suit fall into a reading, we may be encouraged to be pragmatic or keep a closer eye on our finances.

Reading Court Cards

Interpreting Court cards is often deemed the most difficult aspect of tarot reading. Courts represent people who might be part of your current circumstances or your past, or they may have the potential to enter your future. Age can play a part in their interpretation. A Page could describe a child, and a King may signify a wise gentleman. When reading the cards, however, it is worth letting your intuition guide your response. While someone may be in their twilight years, it doesn't mean that their naivete can't be highlighted by a younger member of the Court. Just because we are worldly within business (like the King of Pentacles), we may be less than astute within our personal affairs (like the Page of Cups).

There will be times when the attributes of the Court cards describe yourself, and this is where things tend to get confusing. It is generally suggested that you take a moment to ask your intuition whether the card symbolizes you or someone else, but there will be times when the card can represent both at the same time. For example, the astute Queen of Swords might concern an opponent with a sharp focus. If this is a possibility, then the card could also suggest that you keep your wits about you.

There will be times when a situation can be described by a Court card. Since the Pages are the youngest in rank, they are concerned with new growth and starting out. The Knights, sometimes shown on horseback, are representative of movement. The Queens are nurturers and indicative of care. The Kings, being the highest in rank, are the masters of their suit. As an example, the solid King of Cups is a master of his emotions.

The Court cards will be described in detail further on in this book, but here is a simplified idea of their hierarchy:

Pages

Pages are the youngest member of the Court. They are the students of the tarot, open to learning new things within their world. They can bring messages into a reading. The Page of Cups, as an example, might bring messages of an emotional nature.

Knights

Knights can represent adults within the twenty- to thirty-five-year-old bracket. They suggest movement in a reading because they are generally in pursuit of something. The Knight of Wands could be chasing excitement, whereas the Knight of Swords might be seeking information.

Queens

Queens most often represent mature females. These cards are associated with nurturing. What each Queen nurtures is determined by her suit. For instance, the Queen of Pentacles takes care of her finances and physical attributes.

Kings

The Kings are masters of their environment, exerting authority and experience. They are mature men who have gained wisdom within their element. The King of Pentacles may be a man of financial acumen, sometimes advising others of how best to invest their money.

A Note on Character Genders

⋯•◆◆◆◆◆•⋯

Although Pages and Queens are often depicted as female (though Pages also regularly show up as males, as in the Universal Tarot used in this book) and Knights and Kings are mostly shown as male, they are not confined by their gender in a reading. As examples, the Queen of Cups can accurately describe the emotionally receptive side of a male, and the Knight of Wands can illustrate the ambitious and active aspects of a female. Regardless of the gender of the person used in the illustration (if there is one), these cards reflect personality types and are not limited by the gender of the character depicted.

Reversals

A reversal is a card that is dealt upside down in a reading. When a card is reversed, it can present a blockage or even, at times, reverse the meaning of the card. This can sometimes turn a positive card into a problematic one and vice versa.

Whether or not to read reversals or keep a deck right-side-up when performing a reading is a contested subject. Some readers believe that there is no need for reversed cards because there is an even distribution of positive and negative energy in the deck. Others would argue that a reversal fine-tunes a card and makes its meaning a bit more specific.

There is no "right" way, and as with many elements of tarot reading, it really is up to the reader to do what is comfortable. It is a matter of personal choice. What is best for one reader may not be best for you.

In my interpretations for this book, I have described each card within both a light and challenging context. A challenging position could highlight a reversal or a difficult position within a tarot spread. I have also suggested reversed meanings for those who are interested in using them.

❀ ❀ ❀

2

THE MAJOR ARCANA

The Major Arcana consists of twenty-two cards. Each of these carries a powerful and archetypal image. A Major card will require notice in a reading since it regards grand life changes and opportunities. In comparison, the Minor Arcana, the subject of chapter three, is concerned with filling in the more mundane details in one's life.

The Fool

The Fool stands at the beginning of every story. He is filled with energy and enthusiasm, excited to take his first step into any new adventure. His personality is flamboyant and uncompromising, youthful and innocent. Though he might not always know where he is headed, he is eager to get there all the same.

This tarot character suggests a spur-of-the-moment chance or a time when we'll willingly throw caution to the wind and give something a go. When The Fool enters a reading, he brings a whirlwind of excitement. We might view this card as an unconventional friend urging us to take a risk or walk the less-travelled path. The Fool does not worry over yesterday or live in fear of tomorrow; he is only concerned with the now.

While The Fool can represent the positive results of taking a risk, his zest for life and new experiences can occasionally manifest itself as risky foolishness. This card warns the client not to take silly chances but to look into new issues carefully before committing to them.

The Fool as a Situation

When The Fool arises as a situation, we can expect impromptu events and opportunities to come our way. Whether we have been hoping for change or an unexpected opportunity comes knocking, this card presents exciting chances and fresh starts. This could concern a surprise invitation to take a day out of our usual routine, or even the inclination to liven things up in a relationship.

Youthful wonder is the essence of The Fool, reminding us to approach challenges in the way that a child might. While fear and insecurity could play a part in decisions made at this time, we are also reminded to reconnect with our playful and innocent side. Young and inexperienced people will often feel fear but take on a challenge anyway, and this is the true nature of The Fool.

The Fool as a Person

When The Fool arises as a person, we encounter someone who finds commitment and conformity difficult. As a free spirit, The Fool is motivated by how they feel in the moment and is unlikely to be swayed by rules, regulations, or the making of plans. This is not someone who wishes to be tied down but, instead, enjoys the freedom of spontaneity and living day-to-day.

Though the person represented by The Fool has an inherent youthful energy, the card needn't describe someone who is actually younger in years. All of us have the spark of The Fool within us, whether we are seventeen or seventy. This card could describe someone who is young at heart or even a person whom others believe is having a midlife crisis.

Generally, people depicted by The Fool are fun to be around. In a relationship, their changeable and impulsive nature can be exciting, since each day will likely be different. For those seeking a committed and practical partner, however, the people described by The Fool might not wish to settle down just yet, and their unpredictable nature could become tiresome.

The Fool and You

- Can you remember a situation where you took a chance, regardless of the advice of others, and it paid off?
- Can you think of someone in your past or present who doesn't conform to society's norms?
- Does spontaneity excite or scare you?
- If The Fool whispered in your ear right now, what would he encourage you to do?

Keywords

New beginnings, spontaneity, an unconventional approach, innocence, taking a chance

Reversed: *Risk, childishness, naivete, frigidity, recklessness*

The Magician

In The Magician, we find confidence and certainty. Unlike the free spirit of The Fool, we find a character who is considered and logical in his approach to any given situation. His power is in his ability to affect life, rather than allowing it to affect him.

The Magician is a symbol of skill. He holds within him everything needed to carry him forward to the next step. As a figure connected with magic, we often think of him as someone who can create something from nothing, but in reality, he is only being resourceful by using those attributes he already has.

The Magician is aware of the power he owns, and he knows how to direct it effectively. As an experienced illusionist, he has the luxury of being able to convince those around him that he can successfully manifest his desires and dreams.

The Magician as a Situation

The Magician can represent an opportunity to turn an idea into something tangible. There are times when we may feel as though we don't have the ability to do this, but the presence of The Magician in a reading reminds us of our current resources. Reserves of confidence, enthusiasm, interpersonal skills, or even a good contact might be what's needed to turn a situation around.

Now is a time to believe in ourselves. To take the next step, we must become committed to our beliefs and dreams. This is a time to become focused. Many artists will relate to The Magician, since he can take inspiration and, with the help of his creative tools, turn it into something that others can appreciate in the physical world.

The Magician as a Person

As a person, The Magician represents those who are in control of the world around them. They will display an effective skill set and have just what is needed to take action. While someone like this could come across as arrogant, these people are generally admired for their ability to get the ball rolling and seemingly make something from nothing. Often, it is their confidence that opens doors, and that will convince others they've got what it takes to succeed.

While The Magician does have recognizable power and skill, we must not forget that as an entertainer, he does have a trick or two up his sleeve. As a person in our life, he could show up as a sketchy salesman or someone manipulative. When shown in a negative light, The Magician is open to using his knowledge deceitfully for personal gain.

The Magician and You

- How powerful do you feel at this time?
- What skills do you possess that will help you to manifest an idea or dream?
- Can you think of someone in your past or present whose confidence and charm has gotten them where they want to be?
- Are you using your personal power positively or negatively?

Keywords

Powers, skill, taking action, confidence, resourcefulness, logic

Reversed: *Manipulation, trickery, lack of resources, unconfident, unfocused*

The High Priestess

The energy of The High Priestess can be found deep within us all. While she is inherently a symbol of feminine wisdom, we all possess her gentle touch and passivity, regardless of our gender or whether we choose to embrace it or not.

Whereas The Magician is a symbol of conscious power and outward action, The High Priestess represents the unconscious and inner knowing. While The Magician is outspoken and dynamic, The High Priestess's true powers are in sensing when to say little and listening to her heart.

It is in our subconscious that The High Priestess resides. We may think of her as our gut feelings or inner voice, assisting us with those problems that the rational mind cannot solve. In essence, she is what we call "female intuition," but in a reading, her deep wisdom is not limited to women alone. We all have the ability to tap into our subconscious and draw important messages from its depths.

The High Priestess as a Situation

Within a situation, we may well be asked to leave what we *know* at the door and take a moment to examine how we *feel* about something or someone. We've all had those times when we walk into a room and feel sensitive to the atmosphere that we find there, or we meet somebody for the first time and distrust them instinctually. This is our intuition in action. When we experience a strong feeling about something (whether positively or negatively), this card asks us to acknowledge this response. It is likely that our intuition is eager to pass on a message—if we're willing to listen.

The High Priestess is a card of deep emotion and mystery, so she can often represent those things that are presently unknown. Due to the quiet and passive nature of this figure, her knowledge cannot be forced and must therefore be coaxed out gently. She may signify information or secrets that are yet to be discovered.

The High Priestess as a Person

As a person, The High Priestess describes someone who has a natural connection to their subconscious feelings. She might turn up as the father who knows when something is troubling his child without needing to be told, or the grandparent who magically seems to have all of the answers. In this sense, the wisdom of The High Priestess will be beneficial, and this person could become a much-needed confidant.

Using the inner guidance of The High Priestess is not limited to an emotional situation though. It can be found within the instinct of a businessperson—that guy who always seems to make successful deals based on his gut response to a proposition.

The High Priestess and You

• Can you remember a situation when you rightly decided to trust your feelings rather than listen to the opinions of others?
• Can you think of a current situation where it may be advantageous to be inactive and quiet, rather than forceful and vocal?
• How often do you quieten your busy mind and listen to the small voice within your subconscious?
• Can you think of any friends or relatives who may be wise beyond their years?

Keywords

Intuition, passivity, patience, inner wisdom, mystery, secrets

Reversed: *Ignoring intuition, secrets revealed, an untrustworthy person*

The Empress

The Empress is a figure of physical abundance and creativity. Often described as an Earth Mother, she beholds all that the world has to offer and generously wishes to shower us with its riches.

The tarot's Empress is a symbol of femininity, but unlike The High Priestess, she is sensual in nature and is an active part of creation. Because she is often associated with Mother Earth, every living thing is regarded as one of her children, so it is not surprising that this is often considered a card of maternal protection and instinct. Many readers have interpreted this card as an indication of fertility, and The Empress can still be predictive of pregnancy.

While this card can speak of conceiving a child and it may refer to a birth, its meaning isn't solely attributed to the nurturing of children. The Empress has a hand in all kinds of creation and can therefore be connected to the arts. Whatever our creativity is based around, this figure encourages growth and helps bring about new projects—whether that is the creation of a new painting, the manifestation of an idea, or the first steps within a new business. Many artists consider The Empress their patron, using her fertile and expansive energy to help them in developing their creative ideas.

The Empress as a Situation

The Empress as a situation concerns the evolution of something new. Of course, this could refer to a physical birth, but it might also regard the beginning of a new project, course, or relationship that needs to be carefully nurtured. While The Empress can describe the care we give to others, she can also highlight a need for self-care. Because The Empress is related to our sensory world, she may suggest a need for nurturing the physical body. If our lifestyle has been working against us, The Empress could be encouraging us to think of how it is affecting our health. She may also suggest that we're not drinking enough water or that we need to modify our diet.

The Empress may appear in a reading when we need to express ourselves and our creativity. Although she inspires many an artist, we do not need to be the next Michelangelo to hear her call. Creativity of all kinds is recognized by this card; whether someone is a gardener, decorator, writer, cook, or just want to plant a few flowers in their window box, The Empress surrounds us with her artistic magic at this time.

The Empress as a Person

Naturally, The Empress concerns mothers of all descriptions. However, one needn't have given birth to a child to be a good mother. The Empress considers all living things her children, so the card may describe a person who cares for elderly parents, works within the caring industry, or someone who parents the children of a partner.

The Empress is warm and passionate about the world around her. She is a loving and sensual woman, eager to express herself and look after those she loves, but when in a challenging position, this woman's protective qualities can become smothering. She might be the person who overfeeds her pets, overprotects her children, and doesn't let her offspring fight their own battles.

The Empress and You

- Can you think of someone like The Empress, who has nurtured you and helped you become the person you are?
- How might you tap into your own creative flair?
- Is there a fine line between being caring and being overprotective?
- How can you maintain your physical health?

Keywords

Femininity, motherhood, creativity, nurturing, nature, abundance, fertility, pregnancy

Reversed: *Neglect, infertility, uncaring, scarcity, creative blocks*

The Emperor

The Emperor is a symbol of authority. This man taps into the masculine energy within us all, regardless of our gender, and he helps us to become organized and take control of our personal power.

The Emperor and The Empress are intrinsically linked. Where she symbolizes a maternal figure for most of us, he represents our paternal influence. She is the mother, nurturing and caring, and he is the father, administering rules. Without his guidance, we lack discipline.

Set beside the abundant and warm Empress, it might seem as though The Emperor is somewhat of a party pooper, eager to spoil all the fun, but this is not so. We all need rules and boundaries set in place, and The Emperor can encourage us to change a situation from chaos into order.

When this card enters a reading, it could be questioning our feelings about authority. Are we required to take on an authoritative role, or is The Emperor a force we must adhere to or rebel against?

The Emperor as a Situation

While it is natural to view The Emperor as a person, this needn't always be the case in a reading. There will be times when this figure can show up as a force bigger than any one individual. He might, for example, symbolize a company you work for that enforces rules and procedures. The card is an indication of power, which we can work either with or against, so it is important to acknowledge that, while standing up to a company or large group may be a challenge, it is not impossible.

As a situation, The Emperor may ask us to exercise some discipline. This might be as simple as cutting out distractions and getting on with a job that needs to be completed, or it could describe putting a bigger plan into action. Rules and regulations might appear stuffy or boring to many of us, but they can be greatly underrated. A little order and self-discipline can turn a failure into a success.

The Emperor as a Person

When describing a person, The Emperor is a figure of masculine power. Although he has a caring and fatherly side to his nature, he is more readily recognized for his ability to control and delegate. He could be the boss, but more likely is someone who calls the shots from higher up on the business ladder. We may be aware of his influence, rather than being in actual contact with him.

In a personal relationship, this person has the same tendency to control and exercise his authority as he does in business. Some might find it attractive to be protected and directed by him, but when this card is in a challenging position, The Emperor can become dominant and, at worst, detached from his emotions due to his need for power. Whether he is a lover who wishes to control our every move, or a father figure who won't allow us to grow up, this person can be hard to please when poorly placed in a reading.

The Emperor and You

• How powerful do you feel?
• How would you describe your relationship with authority?
• Where might you instigate control and organization in your personal or professional life?
• Can you think of someone like The Emperor, whose authoritative demeanor can feel intimidating to be around?

Keywords

Power, authority, control, discipline, leadership, paternal influence

Reversed: *Dominant, overbearing, arrogant, undisciplined, disorganized, chaotic*

The Hierophant

THE HIEROPHANT

The Hierophant is often depicted as a religious figure in historical decks—a person here on Earth who has the ability to work as a messenger between us and a higher power. Although traditionally shown as a pope, there is a wide range of different Hierophants in modern tarot, adhering to the many spiritual practices around the world.

Like the worldly Emperor, the Hierophant is also described as a leader and authoritative figure. This card, however, concerns spiritual leadership and often traditional religious views. The Hierophant has his own set of rules, and he could be asking if we are ready to conform and follow them. Do you join in, or will you carve out your own path?

The Hierophant can be a card of comfort to many because he opens his arms to those who find power and faith in his wise words. He is a teacher of morals and values, which has resulted in this card being linked to education and all kinds of educational facilities. If we are willing to learn, then he is willing to teach and share his knowledge with us.

Due to his connection to conformity, this card is also concerned with groups. Whether this is a spiritual group, a workers' union, or a local council, there will be some kind of shared belief or intention that unites its members.

The Hierophant as a Situation

The rules associated with this card could be described as a moral code of ethics, understood and practiced by a group or delivered by an inspirational and revered leader. In many ways, this can keep us feeling safe, since there is often security in knowing that we are not alone on our journey. Joining forces with others and being part of an established society might be something to consider when The Hierophant arrives in a reading.

While this card does deliver a message of group support and wisdom, not everyone will view it in such a positive way. It might stick in the throat of someone who has had a bad experience with organized religion or has felt suffocated by an enforced belief system. With this in mind, it can suggest a need for breaking away from groups of all kinds and encourage independence when in a challenging position during a reading.

At its core, The Hierophant is a teacher, regardless of where and what he teaches. This will be relevant for anyone considering a course of education or who wishes to find a teacher.

The Hierophant as a Person

Naturally, The Hierophant will describe respected religious leaders and gurus of all faiths. When favorable in a reading, this is someone we can approach for support and assistance, but this needn't be in person. The internet has made it far easier for us to connect with motivational speakers and teachers of all descriptions, or we might find our Hierophant within the pages of a self-help book or an online video series.

In personal relationships, The Hierophant can appear as a conformist. This person will have a traditional outlook on the world and may have deep spiritual or religious faith. When in a challenging position, this person could show up either as fanatical about their beliefs or as some kind of evangelist, eager to convert people to their way of thinking.

The Hierophant and You

• Are you a leader or a follower?
• How do you feel about conformity?
• Can you think of a person like The Hierophant, whose teachings inspire and comfort you?
• Is there an opportunity for you to join a group or start some kind of educational course at this time?

Keywords

Tradition, conformity, convention, spirituality, organized religion, groups, education

Reversed: *Unconventional attitudes, independence, lack of morals, corrupt advice*

The Lovers

In modern tarot, there are many fun and interesting portrayals of The Lovers. A large number of them focus on relationships and a union of opposites, but it's interesting to note that one of the historical meanings for the card is that of choice.

When you think about it, what bigger choice do we make than deciding who to take as a partner? For many, choosing to be one half of a partnership means that big changes will occur, echoing throughout the remainder of one's life. Whether we are leaving the comfort of the family home to get married or giving up our single lifestyle to commit to one person, The Lovers can suggest a decision that will dramatically alter our entire world and the people in it.

The Lovers can describe partnerships of all kinds. Though it will most likely signify the potential for a deep and loving romantic relationship, strong friendships and significant business deals may be highlighted too. Deciding to merge with another associate or company should not be taken lightly, since it may entail losing an aspect of direct control. When this card is in a favorable position, successful business endeavors and contracts will be indicated when relevant.

The Lovers as a Situation

For anyone inquiring about the prospect of a committed relationship, The Lovers is a highly fortuitous card and should be acknowledged in a reading. Its message, of course, will depend on its placement. In the area of the past, it will speak of a significant previous relationship. In the present, it will suggest that choices made now will impact our romantic future.

In its most general of meanings, the card suggests the union of two forces. Many depictions of the card will show the marriage of male and female energy but, as we know, this is not synonymous with gender. All loving relationships are covered by The Lovers, and commitment is their overruling quality. Established relationships and those likely to result in marriage or a deeper connection are described by this card. When in a challenging position, The Lovers highlights problematic relationships or couples who have become distanced. In its worst light, the card will promote separation or even the divorce of two parties.

For readings that don't regard love and relationships, this card will speak of an important decision that needs to be made. This will not involve matters of an everyday nature, though, because life-changing decisions will be required, and it could be advisable to seek professional advice.

The Lovers as a Person

The Lovers, when describing a person, shows someone who is romantic. This person is, however, committed rather than fanciful. The Lovers might have romantic ideals, but his or her interest is anchored within realistic goals. If this card depicts someone in our lives, then that person could be harboring ideas of a marriage proposal or a wish for the relationship to become more permanent.

Due to its original meaning, The Lovers suggests someone who can help to make an important decision. While the card may describe someone who is unaware of which path to take, it can also speak of an advisor who can assist them, such as a therapist or marriage counselor.

The Lovers and You

• Are you on the brink of making an important choice?
• How decisive are you?
• Are you considering an important merger or partnership that will create big changes in your life?
• How committed are you to a romantic relationship?

Keywords

Choice, life-changing decisions, love, marriage, partnership

Reversed: Bad choices, difficult relationships, separation, falling out of love, divorce

The Chariot

The Chariot is often referred to as an indicator of success. Storming into a reading, this card concerns movement and triumph, despite those things that try to stand in its way.

The Chariot, being a vehicle, is a card of progress. What makes this a special card is that moving forward is not always easy. Only the luckiest of individuals will manage to get from A to B without having their momentum beset with an obstacle or two, and it is the overcoming of these trials that makes the success depicted here even more impactful for the seeker.

Primarily, this card is one of confidence and focus. It allows us to plan our way forward and consider ways of tackling problems before they consume us. When we know where we want to be, we organize a route. The charioteer, shown in this card, must make sure that his route ahead is clear and ready. For some, this will be a personal process, alleviating fears and strengthening a sense of purpose.

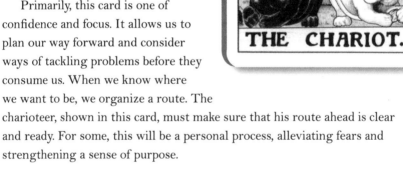

The Chariot as a Situation

As a situation, The Chariot is a card of triumph over adversity. When it arrives in a reading, it will likely concern challenges that can, and will, be overcome. For some, it will provide clarification, reminding them that they have what it takes to be successful, and encouraging them to remain confident in their abilities. This might concern putting problems into perspective, rather than letting fear or self-doubt take control. Whatever lies in the way is surmountable when sprinkled with a little self-belief and courage.

Many modern commentators will associate The Chariot with motor vehicles. In a mundane reading, the card could suggest a car or a means of travel. With this in mind, important journeys and trips may be relevant. It's interesting to note that, when in a challenging position, the card could also regard issues with the roadworthiness of a car or the delay, or even cancellation, of a trip.

The Chariot as a Person

As a person, The Chariot is someone of courage and self-belief. This is someone who is "going places" and doesn't allow fear to prevent them from getting where they wish to be.

While this person might be naturally confident, this card is not only associated with high achievers. We all have the ability to experience the success of this card, so it can describe those people who defeat obstacles against the odds. Whether this is someone who has survived a difficult childhood or a bad marriage, The Chariot highlights a person with the desire to persevere and keep going.

The Chariot, when connected to movement and vehicles, could describe someone whose livelihood is dependent on driving. Taxi drivers, driving instructors, or couriers of all kinds fall under the influence of this card.

The Chariot and You

• How courageous do you feel?
• Can you think of a time when you gained success, despite difficult obstacles?
• Are you experiencing problems with your car, or would a vehicle be a solution to a problem at this time?
• What do you need to overcome to gain confidence?

Keywords

Confidence, courage, overcoming obstacles, travel, success, motor vehicles

Reversed: *Insecurity, recklessness, lack of direction, travel problems*

Strength

Strength, at its heart, is a card of innate bravery and endurance. It most often arrives in a reading to remind us of our skills and capabilities during stressful or difficult times.

When we hear the word *strength*, we likely think of someone who is physically fit and able to fight off adversity with ease. Indeed, in some early representations of the card, you could be forgiven for thinking that there is little more to its message than just that. Most readers will agree, however, that while the card can pertain to being physically strong and healthy, it has a greater association with inner strength and courage.

We've all heard stories of frail people pulling loved ones twice their own weight from burning buildings. We've heard of others who have lain beneath the rubble of earthquakes for days and survived, or tiny babies who've fought to live at the beginning of their life, despite grim medical diagnoses. This is part of what Strength is really about—finding courage during a time of great opposition or fear.

Strength as a Situation

Strength will turn up in readings when we need to tap into our own courageous spirit and face something that intimidates us. We might not feel that we have the bravery to face our fears, but the card advises us to confront that which is intimidating and show that we mean business. In some instances, it might be our ego, reactions, or animalistic desires that need to be gently suppressed—we may need to curb the beast within us, rather than something outside of ourselves.

What we often forget is that strength needn't incorporate aggression. At its heart, Strength is a compassionate and understanding card. It seeks to defuse a situation, rather than arouse it. Mastering our base needs requires patience, time, and trust.

When Strength is in a challenging position, our desires, reactions, and fears are most definitely controlling us. As a situation, there could be problems with aggression or some kind of addictive behavior.

Strength as a Person

As a person, Strength can describe someone with a gentle disposition, but who is far from meek. This is someone who doesn't need to fight with their fists but can win a war through determination and conviction. Strength is not prone to giving up and will keep going, whatever is thrown in their way.

We have all met people like this and we wonder what drives them to keep going. Whether it is their faith, self-belief, or fearlessness, this person has an inner strength that can be very inspiring.

The strong-willed are also indicated when Strength comes into play. Those who can fight an addiction, stay calm in a crisis, or apply resistance when aroused by temptation are all described by this card.

Strength and You

- Do you need to be physically fit to be strong?
- What or whom do you need to stand up to?
- What part of your self needs to be suppressed?
- How can a gentle approach be more effective than an aggressive reaction?

Keywords

Inner strength, courage, conviction, mastering base desires, fearlessness

Reversed: *Weakness, vulnerability, lack of self-discipline, led by urges*

The Hermit

The Hermit pulls away from society and follows his own quiet path. In doing so, he travels deep within himself in pursuit of self-knowledge and understanding.

In many tarot decks, The Hermit is shown as a wise old man, but we do not need to be elderly to appreciate his example. There are many landmarks in life that cause us to reflect and learn. For instance, we may wish to take a little time out between jobs to contemplate our next move, or spend some time alone after the breakdown of a relationship to consider what went wrong. This is most effective in solitude, since it is devoid of outside influence and the opinions of others. There will be many times when we look for an answer externally, but the real message of The Hermit concerns solutions that can only be found within. We may wish to contemplate our own situation and work out how we can change our life from the inside out.

The Hermit as a Situation

We may have reached a time when a little reflection is needed. When The Hermit describes a situation, he suggests that we take ourselves away from the crowd so that we can appreciate a clearer perspective. If we are involved in a difficult relationship, for example, it might be easier to figure out which step to take next and to do so by ourselves, without our partner's influence.

On a deeper level, The Hermit can speak about finding ourselves and discovering what our true motives really are. Many people reach a point when a little soul searching is in order. Finding our own path is part of this card's calling, encouraging us to break away from what society might tell us is the right thing to do and rely on our own counsel.

The Hermit as a Person

As a person, The Hermit can act as a guide. They can arise as an experienced elder or someone who exhibits wisdom beyond their years, but this person will never tell us what to do. The Hermit will simply act as a mentor, encouraging us to trust what our instincts advise and to immerse ourselves in self-discovery.

It is important to acknowledge that this card can speak about being alone. On a positive level, it describes someone who is at one with their beliefs and who is independent. When The Hermit is in a challenging position, however, he can speak of loneliness or, at worst, someone who is ostracized by society. Not everyone who stands apart from the crowd does so by choice. Although the card might highlight a loner, it could also describe someone who is desperate to be part of a group or who might feel lonely after the passing of a partner. If surrounded by difficult cards in a reading, The Hermit may represent someone who wishes to rejoin mainstream society but is unsure of how to do so.

The Hermit and You

• How important is it for you to step away from your social environment occasionally?
• Can you think of someone like The Hermit, who acts as a guide in your life?
• Can you remember a time when you have felt lonely or excluded by others?
• What does the term "soul searching" mean to you?

Keywords

Wisdom, solitude, a guide, stepping outside of society, reflection, soul searching

Reversed: *Loneliness, exclusion, rejection, feeling isolated*

Wheel of Fortune

One thing that most people agree on is that the only certain part of life is change. Nothing stays the same, however much we wish it would. The Wheel of Fortune reminds us that all aspects of life—our personal relationships, careers, and health—are consistently in fluctuation.

Due to its title, the Wheel of Fortune can suggest fortuitous events. While it usually pays to prepare for the future, this card suggests that the universe has its own plan. It might provide blessings, but it can equally turn the tables of good fortune and dish out a run of bad luck.

When this card is in play, it is sometimes best to remember that there are universal powers greater than our own. For example, we cannot change the seasons, however much we might prefer twelve months of summer or a longer Christmas holiday. In this sense, the card reminds us that we must go with the flow, because things will change again eventually.

Wheel of Fortune as a Situation

As a situation, this card can determine a spell of good fortune. It could mean an unexpected bonus or even that we might win some cash in the lottery. For anyone suffering a hardship, the Wheel of Fortune will be a welcome omen, since it offers some respite from difficulty.

Of course, what goes up must come down. The hand of fate can bring fortune, but it can also bring difficulty when in a challenging position. Things may have been going well up until now, but when the card is reversed, it could suggest that we'll become besieged by problems. Whether this concerns household bills all coming in at once, a lack of work, or just the general wear and tear of daily life, the Wheel of Fortune's rulership will only be temporary, so don't worry.

Our reaction to change can be our saving grace or it can be our worst enemy. Whatever the wheel brings, we must accept that there will be things we cannot alter. This does not leave us completely powerless, because we still own our responses. The way we choose to act during times of change will have a great impact on how smoothly the cycle passes.

Wheel of Fortune as a Person

As a person, the Wheel of Fortune can describe someone who is thought to be lucky. Luck does seem to follow some people around, and the card could depict a person who always appears to land on their feet. This could be someone who lives a fortunate life, but it could also highlight those people who seem to glide through problems with ease. They may have a knack for always being in the right place at the right time.

The Wheel of Fortune can also describe a person who bounces between extreme highs and lows. Emotionally, their mood may fluctuate greatly from day to day. This person may appear on top of the world on Monday but is at rock bottom by the weekend. They will make a challenging partner or friend, since it might be difficult to predict their moods. Because they are living a reactionary life, the slightest change can influence their frame of mind.

Wheel of Fortune and You

• Would you consider yourself to be lucky?
• Can you remember a time when you needed to deal with a period of bad luck?
• Do you know someone who always seems to land on his or her feet?
• Why might it be best to go with the flow at this time?

Keywords

Fortune, luck, cycles, fate, destiny, fluctuation, change

Reversed: Resisting change, bad luck, rigidity, feeling out of control

Justice

We can get a pretty good idea of what the Justice card means just from its title. It is a symbol of fairness and karma, often shown by a sword representing truth and a set of balanced scales.

The Justice card, of course, has a connection to the law. In some cases, this will be literal and will regard a favorable outcome in a legal situation. If someone asks about a court case, then the card suggests that it will be dealt with in the fairest way possible. What is considered favorable, however, is very much dependent on where the seeker stands within the question. If the questioner has been unfairly treated, then Lady Justice will surely highlight this; but if they are hoping to get away with something and thinks that a judge might turn a blind eye, they're likely to be disappointed. Justice is the "all-seeing eye" from which we cannot hide.

This card will not always mirror a legal situation. In most readings, its message is of fairness in everyday life and relationships. While it might concern fair decisions made with us as a subject, it will acknowledge those times when we receive praise or reward for those things in which we've invested time and effort.

Justice as a Situation

Justice can arrive to depict fairness. If you have been waiting for a verdict that reflects the truth in a situation, then this card will provide you with the answer you have been waiting for. All of the details will have been carefully assessed and considered and a positive result will be forthcoming.

At its most general level, this is a card of karma. The universe always notices those things we say and do; it mightn't reward or punish us instantly, though, and this is something worth remembering. Those things we've said and done can become hidden beneath time and seemingly forgotten, only to arise months or years later. Everything we experience has grown from its own seed, whether planted yesterday or further back in the distant past. With this in mind, Justice asks us to think about our present behavior and how it will affect our future. This card, when being read as a situation, encourages us to be fair in our dealings. It reminds us to study the facts and put aside our emotional response to what is going on when we make a decision. What choice would be the fairest for all concerned?

Justice as a Person

As a person, Justice describes someone who is fair-minded. In a professional setting, we could be looking at a figure within the legal system: a judge, lawyer, or even a witness, who is required to tell the truth. In everyday life, however, this card could depict a person who can make just and clear decisions, uncolored by emotion or bias.

In a challenging position, Justice can describe someone who is playing unfairly. At their very worst, this could be a corrupt person within the legal system but is more likely to be someone who is trying to manipulate the truth for their own gain or satisfaction. A liar, or someone giving false evidence, could be highlighted by this card when it is in reverse.

Justice and You

- How fair are you being within a current situation?
- Can you think of a time when you have been rewarded for your words or actions?
- Who might you go to if you want a fair assessment of a situation?
- How might your current words and actions have far-reaching consequences?

Keywords

Fairness, balance, legal issues, justice, rational decisions

Reversed: *Injustice, imbalance, prejudice, bias, manipulation*

The Hanged Man

The Hanged Man image may be unsettling to some. It is only natural for us to question how he ended up hanging upside down and who might have tied him there. In most decks, this figure appears to be calm, at ease, and in no distress, so it would seem plausible that he actually placed himself in this position, and for a good reason.

This way of looking at the card is imperative to understanding its meaning. The card, at its core, concerns self-sacrifice. This is not a sacrifice that is inflicted on us but one that we undertake ourselves. When this man (or woman in some decks) hangs upside down, his perception changes because he can now see the world in a completely new way. For some of us, this is a sacrifice in itself—putting our ego to the side and allowing ourselves to see the perspective of others. The world looks very different when we step back and view it like this.

Because of this pause in movement, The Hanged Man will sometimes represent delays. Something we'd been hoping for might take a bit longer than we'd expected. Travel or arrangements will take time or may even become temporarily cancelled.

The Hanged Man as a Situation

When The Hanged Man arises as a situation, he might be suggesting that a period of quiet is required. It might be time to step back and look at proceedings from a distance. Sometimes, we need to look at the bigger picture, and that isn't always easy when we're in the thick of things. Standing back allows us to appreciate the opinions of others or find new ways of doing something. Our initial approach might not be the best, and sacrificing our ego may be an important next step.

We all make sacrifices. Refusing something in the present may well be rewarded in the future. For example, sacrificing a tempting piece of chocolate cake might prevent us from putting on a few extra pounds in the long run;

declining a few nights out will leave us with a little more energy and cash to invest in something more fulfilling. The Hanged Man encourages us to adopt a "bigger picture" mentality. Do we want everything now? Or might a little resistance bring greater wisdom or a more fulfilling experience later on?

The Hanged Man as a Person

When describing a person, The Hanged Man might mean someone who is selfless, sacrificing his own needs or desires for a greater good. This might be the parent who forfeits their own luxuries to pay for their child's education, or someone who gives time to a charity.

As a person, this card can also suggest someone who thinks out of the box and enjoys going against the flow and turning what we understand on its head. An artist or writer may enjoy experimenting with a new vision, choosing to look at the world in an entirely new way. Visionaries of all kinds can be described by this card.

In reverse, The Hanged Man actually becomes upright. When in a challenging position, this card can describe one of life's martyrs—the kind of person who is constantly sacrificing aspects of life and complaining about it. We've all met those people who take on too much and never fail to tell us how heavy the weight on their shoulders is.

A reversed Hanged Man can also describe those people who will not make sacrifices or change their viewpoint. If this card turns up to signify a partner in a relationship, it may be alerting us to someone with a selfish streak who isn't willing to be flexible.

The Hanged Man and You

• What sacrifice, whether small or large, can you make for the better good of yourself or those around you?
• How important is it that you change your perspective every so often?
• Can you think of a situation that is suspended at this time and may not resume for the foreseeable future?
• Can you think of someone like The Hanged Man, who sacrifices his or her own needs for the good of a cause or loved ones?

Keywords

Sacrifice, change of perspective, "bigger picture" mentality, delays

Reversed: *Unwilling to sacrifice, selfishness, stubbornness, martyrdom*

Death

The reputation of the Death card often precedes it. If you have ever seen tarot depicted in a film or television program, chances are that this card came up to predict someone's unexpected demise. This has resulted in it being the most feared card in the tarot deck and the reason why many might naturally be fearful of receiving a reading. It provokes the question that so many people ask a tarot reader before a session—does Death actually mean "death"?

When considering whether the Death card mirrors real deaths, the short answer to the question is yes, but this might not be in the way that you imagine. The card is a symbol of endings, and if you think about it, we go through many changes in life that result in the loss of relationships, jobs, or the end of a particular lifestyle. When two people get married, they experience the death of their single lives but, we hope, this is a happy loss.

Of course, the Death card mustn't be sugarcoated, because not every ending is going to be welcomed. Even so, as a reader for over twenty years, I can tell you that the Death card has predicted the deaths of many more situations and unhappy relationships than it has of people's loved ones.

Everything has a shelf life—our relationships, childhood, jobs, and, yes, our physical existence—it's part of the natural cycle of life. The tarot doesn't aim to frighten us but works to alert us beforehand. If we can see that a life situation has the potential to end, we either are warned or have the chance to alter our ways to prevent that from happening. Isn't that a positive thing?

Death as a Situation

If Death has shown itself in a reading, it suggests that an end is near. If we feel unsettled by the card, we must take a moment to think past our fears and consider those things that are destined to end. Are you working your way to the end of a period of education or a course? Are you feeling too old to drive safely any longer? Is retirement approaching you, or are you changing schools soon? All these situations require an ending if a new chapter in life is about to start.

There will be times when cards recur in our readings. The same card will come up over and over, and this suggests that it has a message for us. Not all of us like change and when the Death card continues to come up, it could be encouraging us to end something that is not making us happy. Quite often, we are aware of what it is we need to quit but we are too scared to make the break. When reversed, Death could indicate our resistance to major life changes.

Death as a Person

As a person, the Death card symbolizes someone who welcomes change and the unknown. They are not fearful of endings because Death knows that a new beginning is right around the corner. That person realizes that, in some cases, we can only start anew or begin exciting new adventures if we say goodbye to those things or people we have outgrown. In some instances, this might be sad or uncomfortable but these people understand that this is necessary for growth.

In a challenging situation, Death may describe the morbid among us. Not everyone can see the positive in a situation, and some might be inclined to fixate on the doom and gloom. When indicating a difficult person, Death suggests those who may have become obsessed with dying or who cannot see a way out.

Death and You
- How might the death of a situation or relationship transform you for the better?
- How might death become a cleansing and liberating experience?
- What ending have you recently experienced?
- How might holding off and postponing change be unhealthy or detrimental?

Keywords
Endings, change, transformation, new beginnings, new direction

Reversed: *Resistance to change, fear of something ending, resisting the new, holding on to the past*

Temperance

In Temperance, we find moderation. The card describes the act of combining the different elements of life harmoniously. This is often easier said than done, since true balance can be difficult to achieve, let alone maintain.

How can we understand what Temperance means in daily life? In many depictions of Temperance, you will find someone mixing the contents of two vessels together. The mixture is no longer one or the other but a combination of the two, a bit like running a bath. We don't fill it with just hot or cold water but endeavor to find a perfect blend of the two.

In a reading, this card might be asking us to reflect on how balanced our life is. Does everything work together harmoniously, or are certain areas becoming overpowering and consuming our attention?

Temperance as a Situation

Temperance will most often arise in a reading to ask us how balanced our life really is. For some, it will be advising that different areas need to be blended more successfully. Are you the person who is so focused on a career that spending so much time in the office is affecting your home life and family? Or, alternatively, are you so absorbed with the party lifestyle that staying out until the small hours is affecting your ability to do your job effectively or complete your studies?

It's important to realize that Temperance does not ask us to stop doing something entirely; it simply suggests that we find balance. For example, the act of tempering food or alcohol intake is not enforced abstinence, because the card suggests that a few drinks or a treat could help us to relax. It also warns against the potential of extreme indulgence.

In some situations, Temperance can concern the mixing of people. Different groups could benefit from being merged, or it could be the right time to introduce a new partner to friends and family.

Temperance as a Person

As a person, Temperance can describe someone with a balanced lifestyle. At best, this person manages to maintain a healthy work and social life with neither overpowering the other. In day-to-day life, they mightn't always eat the healthiest of foods, but their diet is balanced and considered, knowing that having a little bit of what we like can do us good. In a crisis, Temperance does not immediately react, but considers a response and is good at exercising patience during difficult times.

While this might be a state we all wish to achieve, this person could become a little too good to be true. While we know we must drive within the speed limit and that a good night's sleep is preferable to pulling an all-nighter, such caution could become tiresome.

Temperance and You

• How balanced is your lifestyle?
• What area of life do you feel you need to temper?
• Can you think of someone like Temperance, who maintains a healthy balance within his or her life?
• What areas of your life would benefit from being integrated?

Keywords

Moderation, balance, the perfect blend, patience, common ground

Reversed: *Imbalance, impatience, excess, discord, indulgence*

The Devil

Like Death, The Devil is a card that can unsettle new readers and clients alike, and this is not surprising, since some depictions can shake the hardiest of souls. Whether your version shows the overwhelmingly large and hairy Devil of Christian religion, or suggests one of your more personal demons, this card is not the easiest of the seventy-eight to comfortably accept.

The tarot acts as a mirror, and what is reflected is not always light and positive. Some cards, such as The Devil, help to maintain balance within the deck because our experiences, after all, are wide and diverse, negative and positive.

While The Devil may show up as ugly, or even scary, within your tarot deck, it is important to remember that he is not an external force. The Devil, in reality, is simply illustrating the ugly and unbalanced aspects of ourselves—those bits we might not wish to acknowledge, such as materialism, selfishness, or unhealthy desires. In short, he is our eagerness to serve the self alone at whatever cost.

The Devil is not a card to fear, because we all have a relationship, whether big or small, with the temptations of modern life and with our base instincts. The card is a much-needed component of the tarot landscape, because he can remind us that we may have fallen out of balance and become trapped by our darkest desires.

The Devil as a Situation

As a situation, The Devil suggests needs that have the ability to consume us and keep us from maintaining a healthy control over our life. He could show up as food, alcohol, sex, or even a need for attention. It is worth noting that none of these things in moderation are bad, but when we begin to feel controlled by our desire for them, this card will begin to turn up in a reading.

In some cases, The Devil will describe an unhealthy partnership. Even though it can suggest an abusive relationship as a worst-case scenario, it often highlights an unhealthy attachment. What is interesting about this is that we are often aware of it but choose to stay within the confines of the relationship regardless. The Devil does not hold us prisoner; we consciously chain ourselves to these things, aware of how destructive they could become.

The Devil will often turn up to represent the material side of life. He does not refer, however, to money or material possessions in themselves; instead, it might be the status we believe these things will give us, or a feeling of emptiness that we hope they'll replace.

The Devil as a Person

As a person, The Devil can describe someone who is manipulative. Remember that this card has a strong link to temptation and seduction, so the person signified will likely be charming, charismatic, and alluring in nature. Not all Devils have an ugly exterior. In fact, this will probably be far from the truth. Their ugliness is something that resides within and will not necessarily become apparent until we are caught within their trap.

As well as those with manipulative traits, we can also find this card describing those who are easily manipulated. While it can describe those trapped within materialism, consumerism, and feeding a need for status, the card can describe those who have succumbed to an unhealthy or unbalanced lifestyle—in extreme cases, the attention seeker, alcoholic, or sex addict could be highlighted by The Devil.

The Devil and You

- What desire could be out of balance and represented by The Devil?
- Can you think of something that you know is unhealthy but which you continue to stay involved with or connected to?
- Can you think of someone like The Devil, who knows how to wrap you around his or her little finger with little effort?
- What is stopping you from walking away from those things or people that you know are not good for you?

Keywords

Temptation, seduction, manipulation, materialism, addiction, lust

Reversed: *Freedom, independence, walking away from unhealthy relationships*

The Tower

There is little in life that stays the same. Change in itself is what makes the world go 'round, but when it appears unexpectedly, we feel a lack of control and can be left feeling vulnerable and insecure.

The Tower is a card that comes with a reputation. Due to the imagery depicted in many decks, it is associated with chaos and destruction. Most of us would invite change into our life if we could prepare for it, but this card doesn't allow for that. While we may have been worrying about the prospect of an upheaval, the explosive arrival of The Tower is likely to bring one we were not expecting.

When we think of a tower, we imagine something that is tall and strong, but it is not necessarily the construction in itself that keeps it secure. If the foundation beneath the building is shaky or badly designed, that will not protect it from attack.

While The Tower is a much-feared card, it needn't become an entirely negative experience. There will be times when unexpected change will help us to move forward, especially if we have been resisting it through fear or control.

The Tower as a Situation

There is no doubt that The Tower can wreak havoc in our daily life. There will be times when it pulls the ground from beneath our feet and turns our world upside down. For this reason, seeing the card in our future can enable us to prepare. For example, if it sits within the future of a romantic reading, the card could be advising us to assess how strong the foundations of our relationship are. If things are not as tight as we'd like them to be, then a chat with a partner could help weather a forthcoming storm. When signifying the present, it might accurately describe current turmoil or swift and unexpected change that has knocked us off our feet. If we are suffering the effects of The Tower, then the card could be asking us to try and rebuild what has been lost. A relationship or situation may need to be worked on, or in a worst-case scenario, accepted as being over.

Hindsight is a wonderful thing, and after the fact, we may find the experience more beneficial than we'd imagined it could be. The Tower can be seen as a prison: a situation or partnership that many of us are too scared to try and escape from. In this instance, the inevitable steps in and makes the changes for us.

The Tower as a Person

As a person, The Tower can describe someone who may be viewed as unstable. Unlike The Fool, who is carefree and optimistic, the person described by The Tower can be prone to outbursts or might be unable to cope during strife. This can result in meltdowns, erratic behavior, or at worst, aggression.

Generally, the card could describe someone who is hotheaded and liable to blow his or her top when pushed too far. There is an unpredictable nature to their personality, so it might not always be easy to tell if or when this is going to happen.

The Tower and You

• Can you think of a relationship or life situation that is unstable and might not survive a confrontation?
• Can you remember a chaotic change of events that shook your personal stability but which actually turned out to be a blessing?
• How might a lack of change be holding you as a prisoner in your life?
• Can you think of someone like The Tower, who is unpredictable and will blow his or her top when pushed too far?

Keywords

Unexpected change, chaos, disruption, shock, vulnerable structures

Reversed: *Release, ability to start afresh, going with the flow*

The Star

While there are positive and negative attributes to each of the seventy-eight tarot cards, you could say that there are some that have a slightly more positive outlook than others. The Star, a card of inspiration and light, is one of them.

Due to its placement in the Major Arcana, The Star is often associated with hope. If you think about the cards that precede it, this would make sense. After our brush with Death, meeting The Devil, and the shock of the falling Tower, hope is a natural next step. The Star is often depicted with a gentle and feminine energy. It is the light at the end of a dark tunnel and many find it to be both refreshing and comforting within a reading.

This card is often linked to wishes and dreams. Most of us will recognize the link between hopes and the stars, and the card often reminds us that there is a place for dreaming, regardless of recent difficult events or a belief that things aren't likely to improve.

The Star as a Situation

As a situation, The Star is a beacon of inspiration and a promise of forthcoming joy. If we have been through a hard time, it might be easier to give up than put our future in the hands of wishful thinking. We may be fearful of becoming disappointed or hurt all over again, but The Star reminds us that we must never give up. When we ignore her light, we choose to cover the true light within our self. What is life without hope or dreams?

When this card arrives in a reading, we must remember that there is always a way forward. This guiding light is advising us to look to the future, because the past has now been and gone. This might not be easy, since faith alone could leave us feeling defenseless, but The Star advises that it is wholly necessary.

In some cases, The Star will simply concern inspiration. It will represent an idea that breaks through and illuminates a creative block or unlocks a puzzle that has been confounding us.

The Star as a Person

As a person, The Star describes someone who has faith in the future. This may be someone with religious or spiritual beliefs, but generally the card represents anyone who is able to look beyond present difficulties and believes in a way toward a better world.

The Star can concern guides of all kinds—whether this is an astrologer, motivational speaker, or self-help guru. These people will help us to find light amid darkness and a path of hope when there doesn't appear to be one.

In a challenging position, this card could describe someone with a pessimistic outlook. This person may be faithless after being dealt a cruel hand or unable to see opportunities that are currently open to them. Guidance and a new start could be within their grasp, though their lack of hope is preventing them from seeing it.

The Star and You

• What belief or faith keeps you going?
• Do you believe that wishes are granted?
• Can you think of someone like The Star, who is forever hopeful, regardless of previous trials?
• How difficult is it for you to put yourself in the hands of wishful thinking at this time?

Keywords

Hope, inspiration, guidance, wishes, light at the end of the tunnel

Reversed: *Lack of hope, pessimism, unrealistic wishes, faithlessness*

The Moon

Most of us will agree that The Moon is something of great beauty. As a symbol, it is linked to the goddess, is feminine in nature, and is highly seductive. When beneath the moonlight, however, things are not so easy to comprehend.

When this card arises in a reading, aspects of life may become harder to understand and could result in us feeling disorientated. When manipulated by moonlight, we might find it difficult to tell the difference between what is real and what is not. Have you ever woken in the night and mistaken shadows for monsters, or even wondered where you were for a moment or two? When The Moon glides over a reading, it is natural for us to feel unsure of the facts within a situation.

Even though The Moon is traditionally associated with confusion, it is far more than just that. It is under the moonlight that we experience the benefit of darkness. The card encourages us to look beneath what we see in the daylight, and in some cases, use the inspiration found within our dreamtime creatively. The card can provide an alternative perspective of the world—one that might sometimes be strange or obscure, but which can be enlightening when one takes the time for self-reflection and for the creation of artistic ventures. For some, diving deeper into their own psyche will be extremely rewarding.

The Moon as a Situation

When describing a situation, The Moon advises that things are not necessarily how they seem. We must remember that the energy of this card is like a veil of mist that is covering up the truth. It creates an illusion that can be easy to fall for.

It is important to realize that how we see something may be obscured. We may be unaware of what is really going on and could have had the wool pulled over our eyes. If we are feeling unsure about what to do, now might not be the time to act. As with all cards, their influence is only temporary, so it might be advisable to put off making important decisions until a true understanding of the facts is gained.

In a positive light, The Moon might be asking us to examine our feelings. Our reaction to a specific situation may run deeper than we thought, and a little self-understanding could be beneficial. While difficult, this card could be asking us to explore things we've hidden away and find hard to confront. Of course, doing this may be uncomfortable and in some cases could do more harm than good. If we think that the resurfacing of difficult emotions will be helpful but unsettling, the card encourages us to seek the assistance of a professional who can help do this safely.

The Moon as a Person

As a person, The Moon will describe those who have an interest in digging deeper within the psyche of themselves and others. This could manifest as someone who doesn't enjoy surface chitchat but likes to indulge in deep and meaningful conversation. The "amateur psychologist," or someone wishing to know how others "tick,'" could be indicated when this card is in play.

Naturally, The Moon will describe the deceptive among us. Con men and those actively trying to deceive must be acknowledged. If this card is describing someone we know, then it is highly likely that he or she has something to hide. This card could confirm suspicions about a partner or alert us to a hidden agenda.

Not all people signified by The Moon are deceptive, though. Since the card can indicate an expansion of our imagination, artists, poets, and actors could be highlighted. If we take an actor as an example, it is his job to convince his audience that he is someone different from himself when performing. This is an illusion, but within the play, is not negatively deceptive.

The Moon and You

- What masks do you wear with other people?
- Can you remember a time when the bigger picture was obscured and you were unable to see things as they truly were?
- How comfortable are you when dealing with your past and deeper feelings?
- Can you think of someone like The Moon, who is able to pull the wool over people's eyes, whether positively or negatively?

Keywords

Deception, insecurity, confusion, imagination, emotions, feminine energy

Reversed: *Clarity, seeing the bigger picture, unmasking a con man*

The Sun

Whereas The Moon has a decidedly feminine energy and is often associated with the goddess, the Sun is inherently masculine. In fact, the two cards have an important relationship because where The Moon seeks to conceal, The Sun reveals what is truly there.

The Sun is a warm and positive card that is welcome within most readings. We need only think about how uplifting it is to see the sun streaming through our window in the morning or to feel its rays on our back for its vitality to make sense. In terms of our emotional and mental well-being, it is crucial.

The Sun enables us to see clearly. While it can provide a natural boost to our health, it will show those areas of life that have become difficult to see. For example, think of a dark room that has been lit by the sun: you can now see every detail, every speck of dust. In this instance, the card allows those things we were previously unaware of to be highlighted.

The Sun as a Situation

The Sun can suggest a time of warmth and exuberance, so is often associated with victory and success. If we have been working toward a goal, this card will act as a significant reward, allowing for us to feel proud of our accomplishments and celebrate with those around us. If we have been feeling under the weather, then a promise of relief and vitality is expected when this card touches your reading. Whatever you are reading about, The Sun will provide a positive spin on the subject.

While The Sun can naturally enhance our mood, we must remember that it does not pick and choose in what it reveals. If we have been trying to hide something and this card shows up in a reading, it will bring out the truth, warts and all. No matter how we try to hide from it, The Sun is a symbol of a truth that will soon be revealed.

The Sun as a Person

When describing a person, it would make sense to think of those in good physical shape. It may describe someone who is strong and healthy and who enjoys being out in good weather, possibly working as a holiday rep. Laying physical attributes aside, the card will speak of anyone who has a positive attitude and confidence, and tends to look on the bright side of life.

When The Sun is reversed, it can become mildly challenging. The positive attributes of a person described by this card can manifest as arrogance and egotism. It could represent someone who is "too good to be true" or who thinks they are more important or significant than anyone else. You might find this person indulging in one selfie after another on social media, eager to show the world just how incredible they believe they are. This is someone who loves to be looked at and refuses to hide in the shadows.

The Sun and You

• Do you need to spend more time outside, for the sake of your emotional and physical health?
• What do you feel proud of at this time?
• What is the difference between confidence and arrogance?
• How optimistic about the future do you feel?

Keywords

Health, vitality, truth, success, masculine energy, confidence, positivity, fame

Reversed: *Feeling under the weather, arrogance, vanity, feeling unwell*

Judgement

Within the tarot deck, we find a handful of cards that are indicative of change. For some people, these are frightening because they can step in and turn things upside down without warning. Judgement is also a harbinger of change, but it allows us to decide how and when we will modify our lives.

Many see Judgement as a call to action. When the card arises in a reading, it asks us to consider something of importance. In larger spreads, this is likely to have life-changing significance and further-reaching consequences than if we are just giving a reading about the following day. We might see it as a cosmic alarm bell, encouraging us to assess where we are on our life path.

Generally, the card concerns a time of evaluation, where we're reminded that change is necessary. It asks us to think about what we no longer need and what we think is still important for the journey ahead. While this revelation may feel divinely inspired, the practicalities of transformation are in your hands. Only you can decide on how and when you make these changes.

Judgement as a Situation

When Judgement describes a situation, it most often speaks of self-assessment. Due to its title, people can be put off by this card, thinking it concerns negative judgement from others. The judgement suggested by this card is our own, focused on situations we are currently experiencing.

For some of us, the card will provoke an entirely new direction. We may see an advertisement for a new career opportunity that causes us to think about how excited we are about our present job; or maybe something has awakened an interest in a course of study. The ideas aroused by the Judgement card are not always revelatory. In many cases, something simply revives a previous idea or calls for us to think about how content we are.

Not all assessments are as radical as a change of career or relationship, though. For instance, a bout of illness may encourage a new health regime or diet. Bad service from a business could mean that we decide to take our custom elsewhere. We make judgements about what is best for us every day—some are just that bit bigger than others.

Judgement as a Person

When Judgement describes a person, it can have negative connotations. Nobody enjoys being judged, and this card can hint at the judgemental among us. While it can speak of those involved in the legal system, whose job it is to referee, it may concern people closer to us who think it is alright to pass opinion. At best, this person's awareness could be considered helpful, since it may allow us to make necessary and important changes. There is no place, however, for unhealthy critique or condemnation in a romantic relationship or friendship.

At best, Judgement can describe someone who is self-aware, but this assessment of the self must be constructive. It is always commendable for a person to accurately see where they could be going wrong, but constant self-evaluation may become unhealthy or even narcissistic in some people. Noticing what our issues are can be useful, but if we don't choose to do anything with that insight, they are nothing more than self-absorption.

Judgement and You

• Can you think of something in your past that caused you to reconsider your life path?
• How judgemental are you of others?
• What changes do you feel that you are in control of?
• Does it feel worse to be judged by others or yourself?

Keywords

Judgement, evaluation, assessment, change of life path, healthy self-critique

Reversed: *negative judgement, lack of self-awareness, unhealthy self-critique, self-absorption*

The World

The World is the last card of the Major Arcana and, for that reason, is connected to the completion of a cycle.

Depictions of The World vary from deck to deck but most tarot commentators agree that it signifies an ending. Unlike the unexpected ending of Death or an outcome that is deemed to be negative, this card suggests a successful resolution. Whatever the cycle is representative of—a course of education, a job, or a relationship—it leans toward a harmonious outcome, rather than one of failure or difficult closure.

Some readers associate The World with travel. Whereas some of the Minor Arcana look at small trips, this card can speak of international travel or even emigration. Due to modern technology, we have a closer connection to the rest of the world than ever before. While the ending signified by The World is just one part of the overall journey, this card can remind us that we are also just one person among many.

The World as a Situation

As a situation, The World suggests the culmination of an important stage of our life. For example, it might describe the final examination in a course that needs to be passed for you to graduate. It may concern a wedding that has been planned for over a year and represents a gateway into marriage.

While The World is a card of conclusion, it is important to remember that the cycles of life continue. Once graduated, the student undertakes additional challenges: maybe she applies for further studies or takes her knowledge into the workplace. After a wedding, a couple faces new cycles together—maybe moving to a new home or potentially starting a family. Rather than going back to square one, we begin a fresh, new cycle with a greater understanding and experience than we had before.

Once we have stepped over the threshold of The World, we are unlikely to be the same as we were before. It may describe a promotion or honor of some kind that we have been working toward. When this card is in a challenging position, however, our plans could incur delays or setbacks. In reverse, The World does not suggest that we will not achieve our goals: it simply implies that they will take a little more time.

The World as a Person

As a person, The World suggests someone who is experienced and worldly-wise. The card may describe a person of any age who is well travelled or has amassed a respectable amount of life experience. Significant life events or recognizable awards could be part of this.

In some cases, the card could describe someone whose work is connected to travel. This could be a travel agent, a globetrotter, or a student who is taking a year off to travel internationally.

On a general level, the card highlights those who have worked hard to achieve their goals. Since The World is equivalent to the finishing line in a race, it acknowledges not only the achievement gained but also the effort invested in making it to the end. When in a challenging position, those who give up at the first hurdle may be portrayed by this card. Similarly, anyone who experiences success without putting in the work is hinted at when The World card is reversed.

The World and You

• Are you close to achieving something?
• Can you think of a cycle in your own life that you successfully completed?
• Can you think of someone who is worldly-wise or well-travelled?
• How important is it for you to complete something?

Keywords

Completion, end of a cycle, new beginning, success, international travel

Reversed: *Feeling stuck, setbacks, unmerited success, lack of effort*

3

THE MINOR ARCANA

The Minor Arcana consists of fifty-six cards. These flesh out the Major Arcana by filling in a reading with everyday details. While a card from the Major Arcana can advise of a large transformation, the cards from the Minor Arcana can advise of how these changes might take effect.

The Minor Arcana is broken up into four suits—Wands, Cups, Swords, and Pentacles—each containing fourteen cards. Each of the four suits is connected to an element and the most common associations are Fire, Water, Air, and Earth, respectively, which is used in this book. Each suit contains four Court cards, (sometimes known as *people* or *face cards*). The most widely used titling for these are *Page, Knight, Queen,* and *King.*

Wands	Fire	△
Cups	Water	▽
Swords	Air	△
Pentacles	Earth	▽

WANDS

Ace of Wands

The Ace of Wands is a card of new beginnings. As the suit of Wands is associated with the element of Fire, the Ace embraces creativity and passionate endeavors, both personal and professional.

When we think of passion we might imagine a red-hot fire, out of control and burning with desire. Of course, this would make sense, but every great fire must begin with a spark, and in the suit of Wands, the spark is the Ace. The person receiving this card might not yet have set the world on fire, but chances are they have a pretty good idea of how they might.

The Ace of Wands holds within it the potential for new and exciting paths ahead. It could manifest as a new idea, a spark between two people, or the drive needed to get something started.

Ace of Wands as a Situation

When the Ace of Wands describes a situation, it can concern something new and exciting coming into your life. Due to the creative aspect of Fire, this could be an artistic project, but generally it will regard the beginnings of anything that stimulates interest and enthusiasm.

It is important to remember that the Ace is the first card of any suit. This suggests that it is only the first step toward a goal. While the Ace of Wands will inspire us to invest energy something we consider important, it will take old-fashioned hard work to get us where we need to be. Without a little elbow grease, the Ace of Wands is simply hot air.

Ace of Wands as a Person

The person described by the Ace of Wands is exciting to be around. There is a youthful enthusiasm about her, regardless of age, and she will be imaginative and excitable. The individual could be creative or artistic, but also eager to pursue new and exciting possibilities.

Within personal relationships, the Ace of Wands can indicate the spark of attraction. When shown within an individual, it could describe raw drive and sexual arousal. This card could describe urges that are significant in a reading, and therefore, the card could be associated with encounters of a passionate nature or the realization of a person's own desires.

Ace of Wands and You

• What are you passionate and excited about at this time?
• Can you think of someone who is youthful, passionate, and enthusiastic (regardless of age), like the person described by the Ace of Wands?
• What physical effort would be needed to support your dreams and goals?
• How does the passionate flame of the Ace of Wands reflect your own personal relationships?

Keywords

Exciting new beginnings, drive, inspiration, sexual urges

Reversed: *Lack of motivation, blocked energy, male impotence*

2 of Wands

The 2 of Wands is a card of foresight. When we have decided where we want to be, this is the card that will help us get there.

The 2 of Wands concerns planning for the future. It is about taking an idea, some inspiration or a desire, and deciding to move forward with it. This might involve considering which obstacles might present problems or making sure that we have the correct resources or support before we start a project. When this card sits within a reading, it encourages us to take the first steps toward manifesting a dream or physically planning a journey. In some cases, the card will indicate travel or relocation.

2 of Wands as a Situation

When the 2 of Wands arrives in a reading, it can highlight a need for planning. As well as suggesting that it's time to lay down the foundations of a new journey or project, it also asks that we consider all of the things needed for our adventure ahead of time. As an example, this could suggest arranging travel insurance before embarking on a holiday or obtaining the right qualifications for a chosen career.

While the 2 of Wands will often concern the attainment of goals, it can also describe the coming together of two people seeking the same outcome. On a professional level, the card could describe the union of a likeminded business partner; whereas in a personal relationship, it could hint at sexual chemistry or two people who wish to share a joint interest.

2 of Wands as a Person

The person described by the 2 of Wands does not act on a whim. They know where they want to be, but most importantly, they will have worked out how they are going to get there. This person does not allow chance to play a part in their destiny and will try their level best to make sure that all possibilities are accounted for. For much of the time, this person's ability to plan and assess what might be needed is to their credit, but there may be times when they miss out on the moment because they are unable to relax and enjoy it.

The character of the 2 of Wands is that of the explorer, excited about the future and eager to expand their horizons. At worst, they may feel confined by their situation or environment, spending more time thinking about what could be, rather than what is.

2 of Wands and You

• How would thinking ahead help you at the moment?
• Are you planning a trip or thinking of relocating?
• Can you think of someone with whom you share a mutual spark or creative interest?
• Does planning prevent you from enjoying the spontaneity of life?

Keywords

Planning, foresight, travel, creative partnership, sexual chemistry

Reversed: *Lack of planning, feeling stuck, loss of spark in a relationship*

3 of Wands

In the 3 of Wands, we receive the
rewards of an effort. It confirms that
previous investment and hard work is
now beginning to bear fruit.

Many readers refer to the 3
of Wands as the "ship coming in"
card since it often suggests returns
on those things in which we have
invested time. The response will not
be huge but it will provide initial
confirmation of accomplishment. If
we are feeling as though we have
put a lot of energy into a project or
relationship but are yet to see any
results, this could bring great comfort
in a reading and suggest that things
are about to change.

In some cases, this card will
speak of a visitor from afar or even
the arrival of something important
in the mail. Overseas packages could be
significant.

3 of Wands as a Situation

A project or relationship will often take a lot of time to get off of the ground.
Once a direction is determined, the hours must be put in. There will be many
times when it feels as though the investment has come to nothing, but the 3 of
Wands lets us know that we shall soon receive a notable sign that things are
beginning to move forward.

In a professional scenario, the 3 of Wands might concern a payment
showing up soon or new customers or clients. In terms of modern technology,
we may receive new interest on social media, or a professional profile might
increase in size and popularity.

On a personal level, the 3 of Wands could show the results of a diet or
exercise program that shifts a few pounds or builds up muscle slowly. Whatever

we put our energy into will pay us back when this card is sitting in a future position.

3 of Wands as a Person

Everyone loves someone who tries, and the person indicated by the 3 of Wands has certainly been working their hardest to get where they are.

The 3 of Wands could show someone who is breaking into their chosen career and is now receiving significant praise. This person's ships may well have come in, but they remain grounded and humble in their achievements.

We read about stars who appear to have become overnight successes, but we are often unaware of the effort they invest in their work. While this card shows someone who is receiving payment for their initial effort, this person also recognizes that they have a lot more to do before they attain their ultimate goal.

3 of Wands and You

• What have you invested in that you are waiting to see a return on?
• How can you use the spirit of this card to manifest future desires?
• If this card represented a romantic partner, what would they be like?
• What previous work are you currently seeing the rewards of?

Keyword

Initial rewards, a need to keep going, overseas visitors, packages in the mail

Reversed: *Something not turning out as you'd hoped, lost mail, feeling as though you are not getting anywhere*

4 of Wands

Over time, the 4 of Wands has gained the reputation as the luckiest card in the pack. While it might not have the longevity of some of the other cards in the deck, it does suggest a period of time that is warm and stable.

When the 4 of Wands arrives in a reading, it can be a difficult card to expand on because its meaning is so bright, but it is worth remembering that its kindly nature might not be long-lasting. Whereas it could depict a wedding (a traditional aspect of this card) or a honeymoon period, it does not describe the entire marriage. The card reminds us that there is still more work to be done.

4 of Wands as a Situation

As suggested, the 4 of Wands can arise as a marriage but could describe any occasion that is celebratory and poignant. It could mark a promotion after hard work or a graduation ceremony.

In many cases, this card will suggest how we feel. Rather than describing specific events, it will tell us that a feeling of accomplishment is upon us and that it is a good time to take a break. For some, the card will indicate a vacation. For others, it will reflect a period of contentment and security.

In a challenging position, the card could describe those things that are supposed to bring contentment but which have not lived up to expectation.

4 of Wands as a Person

As a person, the 4 of Wands suggests someone with a cheerful disposition. They will see things in a positive way and will appear healthy and happy in the decisions they have made. When dealing with a person described by this card, we will feel secure and safe in their company.

Due to the connection between the 4 of Wands and weddings or functions, the card could concern those who organize events. This kind of person will possess the passionate and fiery aspects of the suit of Wands in their personality, but they have learned to harness it within a business framework.

4 of Wands and You

• Do you feel as though you have accomplished enough to take a break or short vacation?
• Do you have a wedding or event that you need to plan?
• How do the feelings of security and contentment of the 4 of Wands match your own?
• Can you think of a time when organizing a social event proved more trouble than it was worth?

Keywords

Stability, weddings, organized social events, a vacation after a period of hard work

Reversed: *Cancelled event, feeling burnt out, an event or vacation that didn't turn out as you had hoped*

5 of Wands

The 5 of Wands is a card of challenge and instability. Often considered as a card of struggle, it depicts those times when we face obstacle and strife.

While this might sound depressing, it really needn't be. Most often, it is the obstacles in our day-to-day life that help us build up strength and grow. It takes resistance to bring out the best in us, and this is the premise of the 5 of Wands. The card encourages us to exert ourselves and remember our place in the world. Your output is as important as anyone's, so fighting to prove this is the essence of this card's meaning.

5 of Wands as a Situation

Due to the fighting nature of this card, the 5 of Wands will often highlight competitive situations. When it is drawn, it is likely that we will need to prove our worth against a multitude of tasks or even competitors. It could manifest as a job interview that tests us alongside a host of candidates. In a personal reading, it could describe a group of friends who are all jostling to get our attention.

The 5 of Wands will often show a team of people, all working toward a goal. While they might have their eyes on the same prize, they find it difficult to work together but approach the task as individuals. Therefore, ego could be described within the bones of this card, since each person involved feels that their way is the most relevant.

5 of Wands as a Person

As a person, the 5 of Wands describes someone who is naturally competitive. Since the element of Fire involves energy and passion, this person could be sporty, happy to challenge himself. Similarly, they might have an artistic streak, eager to prove their creative worth among their contemporaries.

If the 5 of Wands highlights an opponent, it might suggest someone who always stands in our way or who presents difficulties. As an example, this could be a work colleague who always finds a problem rather than a solution, or who turns a simple chore into a major ordeal.

Because the 5 of Wands is a card of competition, in personal readings the card could describe someone who is a rival, always trying to keep up with the Joneses and trying to prove they are a cut above the rest.

5 of Wands and You

- How competitive are you?
- Can you think of a group of people whom you find it difficult to work with?
- What struggles are you currently facing, and why is it important that you continue to keep fighting?
- Can you think of a situation where it might be more helpful to work *with* a group, rather than against it?

Keywords

Competition, obstacles, rivalry, struggles

Reversed: *Avoiding conflict, lack of passion, focused teamwork*

6 of Wands

The 6 of Wands is always welcome in a tarot reading because it depicts some kind of success. Many people will want to know if a relationship or career development will work in their favor, and this is the card to confirm that.

When the 6 of Wands graces a reading, it not only suggests that something will have a successful conclusion, but also notes the difficulties overcome to get to this place. This is why the taste of victory is so satisfying; there has been much time, effort, and personal interest invested in this accomplishment.

6 of Wands as a Situation

While the 6 of Wands can reflect moments of pride and accomplishment, it could describe specific events within a reading. It might signify passing a driving test, getting good exam results, or landing a new job. Whatever we have given our time to will be rewarded, but of course, this will only manifest from previous hard work.

The success of the 6 of Wands will sometimes be coupled with fame. Of course, it can suggest becoming well known for a skill or award, but on a more general level, the card will depict recognition. This might be a thank-you from a boss for a job well done or the chance to have a piece of work shown in public.

6 of Wands as a Person

As a person, the 6 of Wands suggests an achiever—someone who has a recognized amount of success and who might even be considered an expert in their chosen field. They might be a team leader or someone with a lot of awards or letters after their name. Of course, the kind of person indicated by this card doesn't need to have recognized qualifications; they instead may have a reputation of expertise and experience.

Recognition of all degrees can be found within the 6 of Wands and can suggest a leader of some type. In today's society, this might be a local celebrity or suggest the lofty heights of internet fame and followers. When this card is in a negative light, it could suggest success built from little skill or hard work, or the responsibility of being a role model.

6 of Wands and You

- Can you think of a recent reward or recognition that the 6 of Wands could signify?
- Can you think of someone, past or present, whom you have been inspired to follow?
- What does success mean to you?
- What recent problems or difficulties have you successfully surmounted?

Keywords

Success, victory, fame, recognition

Reversed: *Failure, egocentricity, downside of fame, success without working for it*

7 of Wands

There are times when we feel as though the world is against us. We've all had those days when it feels as though we are battling one thing after another with little reprieve.

The 7 of Wands is a card of obstacle and defense. In a reading, it will describe those times when we must assert ourselves and defend our position. This could happen in a variety of ways: the natural twists and turns of life may have become more trying than usual, or it might be that everyone wants a piece of our time and soul.

Despite the wearing personality of this card, it does suggest that we have a good footing and are able to stay on top of those things that are nipping at our heels. The 7 of Wands reminds us of our strength, and it encourages us to keep going.

7 of Wands as a Situation

The 7 of Wands could suggest a bunch of things that need to be dealt with. These could span personal and professional life. Maybe we need to hold down the responsibilities of a full-time job as well as the requirements of our family and friends.

In a more challenging position, the 7 of Wands can describe the defense of something important. Are you standing up for your children, your opinion, or even your reputation? This card may arise when we are fighting against the tide that is the viewpoints of others.

7 of Wands as a Person

As a person, the 7 of Wands can describe a born fighter. This is the kind of person who will not let others take advantage of them. They are winners because they believe in themselves, and no cause is too large or small for them to take on. This is a good person to have on your side, since they will defend your honor without question, but they can become a difficult opponent to beat. They would make a good activist or defense lawyer.

In a challenging position, the 7 of Wands will describe someone who could be overly defensive. This person might feel under attack when they are not or might take friendly advice as harsh personal criticism.

7 of Wands and You

• What do you feel you need to protect at this time?
• Are you too quick to react?
• When is defense the best form of attack?
• What do you believe is worth standing up for?

Keywords

Defense, standing up for yourself, the upper hand, challenges

Reversed: *Feeling overwhelmed, accepting defeat, being overly defensive*

8 of Wands

The 8 of Wands is a card of movement. Due to the nature of the element of Fire, it regards drive and can push situations forward quickly and release those things that have previously been delayed.

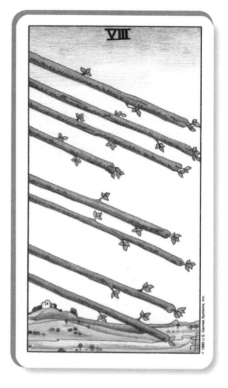

When the 8 of Wands shoots into a reading, it reminds us that something is beginning to gain speed or that action is being taken. In some readings, it will regard travel and relocation.

It is important to ask ourselves how we feel about speed when this card turns up. For anyone waiting on something to start or who is eager to progress, the 8 of Wands will be welcome, but there will be times when we want the world to slow down, too. Holidays or time with someone special may race by, leaving us unable to savor each moment. There will be some people who prefer to ease into situations gradually and might not feel ready to hit the ground running. If we are taken by surprise, the 8 of Wands can feel like a rollercoaster ride.

8 of Wands as a Situation

The 8 of Wands can speed up processes of all kinds. Mail might arrive sooner than imagined, a house sale could go through swiftly, or a deadline might appear closer than it actually is. If we have been experiencing delays and setbacks, this card is advising that things will now begin to move again, and we will become one step closer to our desires.

As well as hurrying situations up, the card is also associated with travel. This might mean a plane trip or even moving. When the 8 of Wands lands in a reading, don't discount vacations or quick trips. An impromptu weekend away might be in the cards.

8 of Wands as a Person

The 8 of Wands describes anybody who is out and about and on the move. Within work, this could be a courier, delivery person, or traveling salesman. If the subject of the reading is the kind of person who is always dashing between one place and another—dropping off the kids, getting to work, doing the shopping, and walking the dog—then *that* could well be the person the card is reflecting.

An athlete might be represented by the 8 of Wands, since the card reflects both their drive and ability to move at great speed.

8 of Wands and You

• Do you thrive on movement and change, or do you find it unsettling?
• Are you planning a trip or vacation at this time?
• If you feel stuck in an area of your life, what would it take to get yourself moving again?
• Can you think of someone who is constantly on the move and doesn't slow down? What is the benefit and detriment of being like this?

Keywords

Movement, speed, travel, relocation

Reversed: *Feeling stuck, delays, not feeling ready for change*

9 of Wands

The 9 of Wands is a card of
perseverance and staying power. It
reminds us of how much strength
we still have in reserve, regardless
of whether we feel tested or have
suffered a disappointment or two
along the way.

The 9 of Wands suggests that we
still have strength to draw on, if we
should need it. While we might feel
worn down by the stresses of daily
life or the obstacles encountered
in a situation, this card encourages
us to keep going. Things are near
completion, and it might take just one
last push to get us to where we wish
to be.

With this card comes a question.
It asks us how important it is for us to
reach the end. In some cases, it might
make sense to carry on, but in others,
we might wonder if we've fought enough already. Within the spirit of the 9 of
Wands is a moment of assessment. If the fight we are involved in is worthy of
our effort, then this card suggests that we must continue.

9 of Wands as a Situation

The 9 of Wands concerns any outcome that one has been working toward
against difficult odds. In some cases, it might be health-related, suggesting
a period of time where we must keep going, though we feel ready to drop.
In others, it will describe those times when a journey (whether physical,
emotional, or mental) has been fraught with setbacks, but we know that we
must continue.

There is a protective side to the 9 of Wands. Due to the amount of energy
invested already, it will regard those people and things which we wish to
defend. If we have been involved with a project that we are deeply passionate

about, this card could advise us to persevere and nurture this creative baby until it is strong enough to succeed on its own. Artists, filmmakers, and writers will all understand the trials involved in bringing a creative project to fruition.

9 of Wands as a Person

The 9 of Wands describes someone with dedication and perseverance. This person does not understand what it is to give up, since they are always prepared to push on through. They'll give every drop of their energy, regardless of what life throws in their direction.

Perseverance can be an admirable quality, but when this card lies in a challenging position within your reading, it could suggest someone who just doesn't realize when they are beaten: this could represent the wounded soldier who continues to push forward and fight for a cause that may no longer be worth fighting for.

If the person described by the 9 of Wands believes in something, they'll act like a dog with a bone. Many of life's greatest activists have understood the spirit of this card, since they have fought tooth and nail for a cause, even at the cost of their own personal well-being.

9 of Wands and You

• Can you think of a time when you pushed through adversity to reach a goal?
• What does the term "wounded soldier" mean to you?
• How might you determine when a cause is no longer worth fighting for?
• Can you think of a well-known person who has fought their way to the bitter end, regardless of how difficult it was to do so?

Keywords

Perseverance, dedication, resources of strength, can-do attitude, defense

Reversed: *Defenses are down, giving up, weakness*

10 of Wands

The 10 of Wands is traditionally seen as a card of responsibility and it can weigh heavily on the bearer. Most often it will appear toward the end of a process. The end may well be in sight but the toll it has taken is noticeable.

When this card enters a reading, it speaks of burden. It's likely that we are feeling overloaded and are beginning to buckle under the strain of multiple responsibilities. While the Wands in this card will feel overwhelming, they could be made up of a variety of different things. These individual obligations might not be particularly draining in themselves, but as a collective, their weight might be too much to bear.

The 10 of Wands asks how might it be best to carry the load. In some cases, it will suggest delegating some duties to others or even letting them go altogether.

10 of Wands as a Situation

As a situation, the 10 of Wands will describe the culmination of duty and responsibility. We may be feeling overwhelmed by too many social arrangements or chores, or we may have more work to do than usual. Dealing with a family, social life, career, and other people's problems could be affecting our well-being and ability to function as we normally would.

In a reading, the 10 of Wands need not be just physical. Emotional worries can overwhelm and might need to be offloaded. We may need to chat with a professional about what is on our mind, as releasing a few concerns could well do the trick. When the 10 of Wands arrives in a reading, the old adage of "a problem shared is a problem halved" makes a whole lot of sense.

10 of Wands as a Person

The person described by the 10 of Wands will likely feel the weight of the world on their shoulders. While they might be overwhelmed by their own problems and responsibilities, they won't think twice about adding everyone else's troubles to the mix. In some cases their support will be appreciated, but often they'll collapse under the emotional strain of trying to be a rock for too many people, and nothing will get done.

This 10 of Wands character will always be willing to help, but there may be times when their personality can be as wearing as the load they feel they are carrying. In a reading this card may show up as someone who fails to appreciate the lighter side of life and may well believe the proverbial cup to be half empty, rather than half full.

10 of Wands and You

- Are you feeling as if you have the weight of the world on your shoulders right now?
- Write out a list of your personal responsibilities. Are there any you could delegate or drop?
- Do you readily worry about other people's problems or say yes to things you know you'll be unable to adhere to?
- Can you think of someone who constantly appears to be bogged down by stresses and strains? What would you recommend to them?

Keywords

Burden, feeling overwhelmed, pressure, responsibility

Reversed: *Delegation, avoiding responsibility, walking away from problematic situations*

Page of Wands

The Page of Wands is the youngest member of the Wands Court, so it is likely that he or she will, at times, represent a child in a reading. If this is the case, this youngster will possess a youthful and enthusiastic drive, eager to become involved with their environment and get started on the next adventure. They do not enjoy sitting around for long and are usually brimming with energy and creative solutions to problems.

Page of Wands as a Person

Due to their age, the Page of Wands may be short of experience and, while they have great reserves of energy and motivation, this can sometimes hold them back. In some situations, they will try to run before they can walk, and this can lead to setbacks or knock down their confidence.

Of course, the Page of Wands can describe someone of any age. From time to time, there is benefit in seeing the world through the childlike wonder of this card, and it is this Page's spark that encourages us to get things moving. While the Page of Wands doesn't have all of the answers, and a little thinking and foresight may be needed, their drive is necessary before any relationship or project can get underway. We could spend weeks and months thinking about how something might manifest, but we all need that initial motivation. That is the essence of this tarot character's personality.

Page of Wands as a Situation

Traditionally, Pages are often viewed as messengers. Because of the nature of Fire, we may experience good news arriving quickly and it could foretell something exciting ahead. Because of the speed associated with the element, it would likely be sent through email, text message, or something similarly speedy.

Generally, the Page of Wands will signify new beginnings or the start of something. It is most likely that the card will be connected with something we are enthusiastic about and eager to get off the ground. Whether connected to our personal or professional life, this young spark will arouse our interest in something new; whether it has the ability to stand the test of time will not be certain until we try it.

Page of Wands and You
• What excites and motivates you at this time?
• Can you think of someone who exhibits the youthful and enthusiastic traits of the Page of Wands?
• What might be the danger of not thinking something through before jumping in feetfirst?
• How might you put the energy of this youthful Page into something useful?

Keywords
Childlike enthusiasm, adventurous, spirited, good news

Reversed: *Lack of motivation, pessimism, fearfulness, difficult news*

Knight of Wands

The Knight of Wands is associated with both movement and enthusiasm. Since he (though the knight can represent a female) has the spirit of Fire racing through his veins, he is a spontaneous and excitable figure, eager to catapult himself into those things that interest and arouse him.

Knight of Wands as a Person

All of the Knights are connected to movement and therefore the pursuit of something. Because the Knight of Wands is ruled by the element of Fire, he is driven by passion and a need to experience the world around him. As a professional, this makes him a great person to have around us because his enthusiasm can be magnetic and he is quick to inspire. If you want someone to create a sense of excitement or get everyone motivated, then this is your guy.

As a lover, this young man is as in demand as he is in his professional life. Known for being charismatic, daring, and energetic, he can make an exciting partner and will be attractive to many. There is, however, a catch. The Knight of Wands, within personal and romantic relationships, will unlikely stay long. He will try his best to charm and seduce you, but the likelihood that he will stick around is slim. Many will fall under his spell and try to tame him, but this is not possible. If you are looking for a fling or a little excitement, he is perfect, but if you want this Knight to commit, you're likely to find yourself disappointed. This young man doesn't settle easily.

Knight of Wands as a Situation

As a situation, the Knight of Wands can symbolize changes and relocation. Because of his element, this will likely be fast and could involve travelling far and to somewhere exotic. Quite often, those receiving this Knight as a situation might be unprepared for his arrival, and the changes he brings might be difficult to adjust to. He could be advising us to take a trip we'd not expected, but it is likely that we'll have little time to pack, let alone prepare.

When the Knight of Wands arrives as a situation, he could be asking us to act as he does. He could be encouraging us to make a move, rather than sitting back and doing nothing, or advising that we direct our energy toward our goals. While his advice may be relevant and well timed, caution must always be noted. The Knight of Wands is usually in a rush to get where he wishes to be and this card, when in a challenging position, may be asking us to stop for a moment and make sure that we have a sound plan in place beforehand.

While exciting, the Knight of Wands lacks long-term commitment in both professional and pleasurable pursuits. He may turn up in a reading to suggest someone is throwing themselves from one project to another or jumping between relationships, unsure of where they eventually hope to be.

Knight of Wands and You

- Are you in need of some excitement in your life?
- Do you have a problem with committing to one idea, job, or partner?
- Can you think of someone like the Knight of Wands, who is inspiring, optimistic, and exciting to be around?
- Do you have itchy feet and wish to travel or relocate?

Keywords

Enthusiasm, inspiration, excitement, fast movement, travel abroad

Reversed: *Commitment issues, laziness, impatience, egotism, rushing*

Queen of Wands

The Queen of Wands is a strong, independent woman. Known to be both sociable and caring, she can be found at the center of most communities, inspiring and helping to bring groups of people together.

Queen of Wands as a Person

All of the Queens are nurturers at heart, but each has their own personal way of interacting with their environment. The Queen of Wands is a people person and often takes it upon herself to coordinate and supervise the running of a project. She enjoys being active, both supervising and participating in her role. The active part of her personality will get things done, and she is respected for her many accomplishments and dependability.

Many look up to the Queen of Wands because she appears to balance her different responsibilities with ease. This is the woman who runs her own business, drops the kids off at school on her way to the office, fulfills her role with the Parent Teacher Organization, but also finds time to meet with her friends for a glass of wine and catch up for an hour over the weekend. What is commendable about this lady is that she manages to maintain all of her responsibilities and none are neglected.

As a soul of Fire, the Queen of Wands is passionate, creative, and extremely sociable. When challenged, however, these aspects of her personality can be used in defense. When cornered, she will be fiercely protective, and if attacked, has enough social support to ostracize her detractor. This is not necessarily a negative quality, because she is certainly a force to be reckoned with, but it might be worth remembering that she can be a vengeful and strong opponent if you plan on confronting her.

Queen of Wands as a Situation

As a situation, the Queen of Wands may well concern social matters. She may encourage us to act as the voice of our community or manage a group of people. This could take effect at work but it might also be required within a group of friends or social club. Not everyone has the confidence or natural ability to facilitate a group or inspire, so this card could suggest that such a personality is required. The Queen of Wands is a good mediator and her positive can-do attitude will get the job done. Do you see yourself as someone who might follow in her footsteps?

Due to the creative side of the element of Fire, the Queen of Wands could be indicating that we need to nurture our creativity. Whether this is through art, music, or dance, as examples, the card could be asking that we think of ways in which our creative talents can be developed.

Queen of Wands and You

• Can you think of someone like the Queen of Wands, who is the hub of his or her community?
• How good are you at balancing the different elements of your daily life?
• How confident do you feel at this time?
• How do you react when you don't get your own way?

Keywords

Confident, independent, sociable, protective, creative

Reversed: *Vengeful, catty, insecure, jealous, reactive, bullying*

King of Wands

The King of Wands is a creative and driven man. He has worked hard to get where he is, and in maturity, uses his experience to direct others and delegate. He is someone who is respected by many, whether they are personally connected to him or admirers from afar.

King of Wands as a Person

All of the tarot Kings are masters, but it is still important to remember that the essence of this King, the element of Fire, still runs through his veins. He has been where the younger Courts have been and can empathize with their need for excitement and haste. Through experience, however, he knows that there are times when it is beneficial to control both. As a person, this man can tap into new and profitable trends and can also foresee ways that they could be used to his advantage, with a little time and planning. This makes him a professional and enterprising businessman.

The King of Wands is a shining light of inspiration for many. He is generous in his dealings and in his personal life can be a warm family man. He is eager to assist others on the path to the top and can make a caring and fair boss.

When in a challenging position, the King of Wands might be so out of reach that he lacks a hands-on approach. While he will still inspire, he might be difficult to contact and won't return emails. At worst, he can be egotistical and arrogant, believing that his wide experience allows him a luxury of better judgement than your own.

King of Wands as a Situation

As a situation, the King of Wands could be asking that we find a way of mastering our enthusiasm or creativity. If we have been floating through life without a purpose, this card might suggest that it's time to get our act together and find a way of challenging our interests and creative ventures. On a personal level, we may be encouraged to knuckle down and find some direction. Our wayward days may be limited, and it could be time to consider responsibilities.

The King of Wands can be counted on when we are feeling lost. As someone who has refined his own talents and needs, he is in a good position to advise us and help us find a new direction. It's worth noting that this King mightn't always inspire or guide from within our immediate circle. Although he might be a sports coach, father figure, or boss, he could manifest as an experienced motivational speaker, a wise elder, or a well-known spiritual figure. This, however, doesn't weaken his message and teachings. The King of Wands has the ability to inspire and offer support through a wide range of different sources, because he understands the power of the media.

King of Wands and You

• How might you control or channel your passions, desires, and interests for your greatest long-term benefit?
• Can you think of someone in your present or in your past who has directly motivated and guided you toward success?
• How might you inspire others by sharing your own experiences?
• Can you think of someone who has from a distance inspired you through their writing, work, or teachings?

Keywords

Leader, motivational, inspiring, courageous, adventurous, warm

Reversed: *Egotistical, overbearing, inflexible, arrogant*

CUPS

Ace of Cups

Within all Aces, we find the beginning of something. In the Ace of Cups, we witness the unfolding of a new emotional situation or encounter. The element of Water relates to the realm of feelings, so can therefore touch on chapters of life that can become both emotionally satisfying and challenging.

The Ace of Cups is most often depicted by a single cup, symbolizing the emotional seed. It can indicate a fresh start within our emotional life and will often predict the beginning of a romantic interest or partnership. Since this is the first card of the suit, its meaning is relatively neutral. While it opens both our heart and mind to the potential of love, it cannot depict how a new relationship will eventually turn out on its own.

Ace of Cups as a Situation

As a situation, the Ace of Cups represents an offer. Within romantically based readings, it can manifest as the first stirrings of emotional interest. Has someone caught your eye recently, or might they have made the first move?

For anyone who has been previously wounded in a relationship, the promise of the Ace of Cups might not be easy to accept. Although it can symbolize the romantic interest of someone new, they may find opening their heart after a painful encounter to be difficult. For the Ace of Cups to turn into something deeper, we must first make room for it. In some cases, we may need to work on our self-esteem and lay the past to rest before we can open ourselves to new opportunities.

In nonromantic readings, the Ace of Cups will signify the beginnings of friendship, our emotional investment in our work, or even the birth of a child. If you find the Ace of Cups within a work-related reading, it will likely encourage you to either find a love for what you do or consider a career in something you love.

Ace of Cups as a Person

The person described by the Ace of Cups will be happy to extend their hand and heart in a given situation. This is not the person who helps you because they feel they ought to, but because they care. The card can highlight someone within a caring profession who is paid to look after others, but it can describe anyone who happily puts the well-being of others before their own. Compassionate people of all kinds will be represented by this card, and in a reading, the Ace of Cups will alert us to someone who really cares about us.

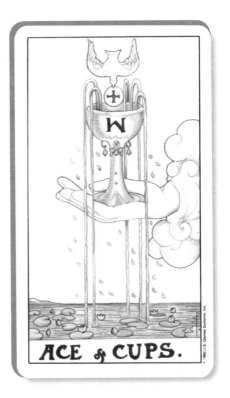

Since the Ace of Cups is no more than a seed waiting to grow and bloom, the card can represent youthful and romantic souls. These people will be sensitive, enthusiastic, and likely to openly express their emotions within their art or through creative writing.

Ace of Cups and You

• How open are you to new love or friendship at this time?
• Do you love the work that you're currently involved in?
• How might you best express your emotions?
• How might you extend the hand of love and care to someone in your life?

Keywords

New emotional situation, the stirring of feelings, opening of the heart

Reversed: *Closed or blocked heart, unrequited love, repressing emotions*

2 of Cups

In the 2 of Cups, we find union. Since
this card sits within the element of
Water and the realm of emotions,
it suggests the blossoming of new
relationships but could also depict
an existing partnership that requires
your attention.

The 2 of Cups can signify a
romantic connection, but when it does,
it will highlight the early stages of a
romance. It may foretell a potential
lover or a significant meeting that is
soon to arise. In this sense, it can stir
romantic feelings between two people
and indicate a first date or mutual
attraction.

While the 2 of Cups can sometimes
suggest our first steps into romantic
union, it will describe partnerships of
all kinds. It has the capacity to include
the mutual care of a friendship and the
coming together of like-minded business partners.

2 of Cups as a Situation

As a situation, the 2 of Cups brings people together. Due to the nature of the
water element, this usually shows up as a heartfelt connection. For anyone on
the lookout for a romantic partner, the 2 of Cups will be a welcome sign: the
card could describe a new person set to enter your life or the deepening of an
existing connection.

For those already in a relationship, the 2 of Cups can encourage getting to
know each other all over again. Maybe a second honeymoon is on the horizon,
or learning to love each other again after a setback will be relevant. Even in the
best of relationships, a couple might need a helping hand. The 2 of Cups may
ask us to compliment our partner, organize a date night, or spend time listening
to how their day has been.

In a work-related reading, the 2 of Cups heralds important partnerships, where new business agreements and contacts will be relevant. Maybe we will become united with a company, employee, or colleague whose interests are closely matched to our own.

2 of Cups as a Person

As a person, the 2 of Cups can symbolize a friend or someone who has our best interests at heart. This person is trustworthy, sensitive, and in touch with their feelings. They will be eager to support us.

The person depicted by the 2 of Cups may be a good friend, a sibling, or even an admirer. They are interested in sharing their personal feelings and wish to help us through difficult times. This card does not describe a fair-weather friend, but rather someone who will be there when the going gets tough.

2 of Cups and You

• What do you bring to new and existing relationships?
• Can you think of a current relationship that is starting to blossom?
• How can you rekindle a friendship or romance that has become tired over time?
• Can you think of someone in your life with whom you share an emotional connection?

Keywords:

Friendship, partnership, beginnings of romance, attraction, shared feelings

Reversed: *Relationship problems, disloyal friend, unrequited love*

3 of Cups

The 3 of Cups represents our social community. It can highlight a group of friends, extended family, or even neighbors.

Since the 3 of Cups brings groups of people together, it will likely suggest public events and parties. Due to its association with celebrations, the card can forecast family get-togethers, birthday parties, and anything that encourages loved ones to meet up and enjoy one another's company. In some cases, it will ask us to let ourselves go and enjoy time spent with those around us.

3 of Cups as a Situation

When the 3 of Cups arrives in a reading, it might predict an invitation of some kind. Maybe we will receive an invitation to a wedding reception, a school reunion, or just a simple night out with friends. If you have been feeling out of sorts of late, the card will remind you that there are people a stone's throw away who are willing to help out, and it could suggest that you organize a get-together.

Traditionally, the 3 of Cups suggests celebrations of all kinds. Depending on where it sits in a reading, the card might hint at things that are soon to be celebrated—such as the passing of a test, a birth, or a new job—or those things already accomplished.

3 of Cups as a Person

As you might expect, a person represented by the 3 of Cups will be fun to spend time with. While they could be a member of your family, a friend, or someone we socialize with after work, this card will likely be an acquaintance or someone we know less intimately than a person described by the 2 of Cups.

As a person, the 3 of Cups suggests someone who enjoys socializing and surrounding themselves with people who know how to have a good time. When this card is in a challenging position within a reading, this person may well put their social life above all else, neglecting other responsibilities. While socializing and organizing events could be an aspect of their career choice, the darker side of the 3 of Cups can be overindulgence or someone whose personal life is getting in the way of their health or work.

3 of Cups and You

- When was the last time you let your hair down or had a night out with friends?
- Can you think of someone who is the life and soul of every party?
- Make a list of the different social groups you are part of and note how they are different.
- In your life, what is worth celebrating today?

Keywords

Celebrations, community, parties, get-togethers, social life, groups

Reversed: *Isolation from a group, burning the candle at both ends, feeling unfairly treated*

4 of Cups

The 4 of Cups is often associated
with stagnation. The suit of Cups
is ruled by the element of Water,
and, as we know, water does not like
to be constricted. It loves to flow.
In this card, we have hit a place of
dissatisfaction. We might not be
happy with what we have got, but
we are blocking the potential for
change, too.

We've all experienced ruts within
daily life. The 4 of Cups recognizes
these blockages, but it can also creep
into readings when we need just a
small shake-up to unlock a major
change. Traditionally, this card is
connected to apathy and boredom.
While we might not be happy with
where we are at, we are also blocking
inspiration or new ideas from reaching
us. In some cases, we might become
so consumed by what is not working that we miss an opportunity to get
ourselves out of our current situation.

4 of Cups as a Situation

The 4 of Cups will arise in a reading when we are feeling discontented with
what we have. It could mirror feelings of disappointment or something that
has not met with our expectations. As an example, this card might turn up for
someone who has spent a year organizing their wedding, preparing every last
detail, but then experiences the blues once it is all over and done with.

When this card is present, it can suggest that our view is too narrow. While
we are absorbed by our discontent or apathy, we fail to notice those things that
could relieve us from it. This card asks us to regain control and look at the
bigger picture. A solution to our problems may be within grasp, but we will not
find it by closing ourselves off from other people or new ideas.

4 of Cups as a Person

The 4 of Cups, when describing a person, will signify someone who feels that what they have is not enough. Have you ever met someone who appears to have everything but is still not satisfied, or is obsessed by what they are getting out of a situation without thinking of those around them?

On a deeper and more serious level, the 4 of Cups can indicate depression or a lack of energy and motivation. The card still depicts someone whose thoughts are centered on the self but who, due to circumstances, is unable to break from the pattern. For this kind of person, venturing outside of their world one step at a time would be the way forward. In this case, professional assistance would be a necessity.

4 of Cups and You

• Have you cut yourself off from those around you?
• What opportunities or inspiration might you be missing out on?
• What could you do to ease yourself back into the world?
• Why might you feel disappointed or apathetic at this time?

Keywords

Apathy, boredom, discontentment, missing out on opportunities

Reversed: *Depression, self-absorption, reaching out to others*

5 of Cups

We cannot truly appreciate the highs that life has to offer without experiencing the odd low too. The 5 of Cups reflects the emotional setbacks and feelings of loss that we all encounter from time to time.

The 5 of Cups cuts a figure of disappointment. Traditionally, it speaks of sadness; it can indicate relationship breakups, and it confirms grief. But while its outlook may appear bleak to most, its potential is heavily dependent on the outlook of the person being read for. While they may have suffered losses, either subtle or significant, the 5 of Cups encourages them to look past their difficulties and find faith in the future.

The 5 of Cups by no means diminishes the problems we have faced already. In fact, it asks us to acknowledge them, because moving forward without doing so is impossible. For those who feel stuck in an emotional rut, however, this card advises them to adjust their mind-set and consider those things they have to look forward to in the future.

5 of Cups as a Situation

As a situation, the 5 of Cups will describe emotional bumps in the road. Relationships do not always run smoothly, and this card could reflect a recent breakup or even the prospect of one. Someone may have deeply hurt our feelings, or the absence of a loved one could be challenging.

When this card sits within a reading that isn't emotionally based, the 5 of Cups could reflect mistakes that are hard to move on from, regret, or even embarrassment. Something will have disrupted the harmony within a situation, leaving us stuck and unable to decide on a next step. In readings concerning business, bad deals might have been made or significant contacts, accounts, or money may have been lost. Although the subject isn't built around the heart, the stresses brought about by the 5 of Cups could cause emotional turbulence.

5 of Cups as a Person

We've all met a "5 of Cups" personality in our time. When asked if the cup is half full or half empty, they'll always go for the second option.

While the 5 of Cups can describe someone who has been through their fair share of grief, it sometimes highlights a personality who chooses to dwell on the negative side of a situation. This person may be difficult to hang around with, because their pessimism can become infectious and bring the general mood down.

We cannot deny that a person described by the 5 of Cups may have very good reason to feel under the weather or could be suffering from a spell of depression. Their inability to seek future happiness and concentrate on past disappointment should not be ignored, and this card could suggest they need to seek guidance from a health care professional.

5 of Cups and You

• Are you finding it difficult to look past a relationship breakup or some kind of emotional loss?
• Make a list of five things that you have to look forward to in your future.
• Can you think of someone who always decides to concentrate on the negative aspects of life, rather than the positive?
• How can you alter your view of a difficult situation for the better?

Keywords

Emotional loss, disappointment, upset, relationship breakdowns, depression

Reversed: *Faith in the future, appreciation of what we have, not acknowledging emotional pain*

6 of Cups

The 6 of Cups is a card of the distant past. For many, it will stretch right back to childhood and the things experienced then. Of course, while this card has a positive vibration, we all have different childhood memories, and one's own personal experiences will color their understanding of the 6 of Cups.

How we view our early life is greatly influenced by youth and naivete. Because of the childlike essence of this card, the 6 of Cups can sometimes alert us to situations where we might become easily deceived in the present. On the flip side, there will be situations and opportunities that require us to be playful and less analytical. The 6 of Cups, when positively aspected in a reading, can encourage a lighthearted attitude.

6 of Cups as a Situation

As a situation, the 6 of Cups will refer to things set in the past. In some readings, it will ask us to delve into our past experiences because the answer to a present problem will exist there. The card could refer to a person in our past who holds the solution to a present problem, or it will advise that we retrace our steps to locate something we might have missed.

Due to its connection to the past, the 6 of Cups can refer to people we might not have seen in some time. The card will often bring an old flame into the present or represent an invitation to a school reunion.

6 of Cups as a Person

With the innocence and essence of a child, the person described by the 6 of Cups is childlike and full of wonder. This can be refreshing, since their optimism and vitality can pull us from the clutches of modern-day strains and stresses, encouraging carefree pastimes and asking us to abstain from responsibility.

As well as describing children who may be relevant to the seeker, the 6 of Cups can describe those of any age who have imaginative personalities and who are open to new experiences.

In more challenging situations, the 6 of Cups can describe those who do not wish to grow up and take responsibility, or those who continually live through past experiences. While it is healthy to reflect or throw caution to the wind on occasion, neither is advisable for a prolonged amount of time.

6 of Cups and You

• Do you need to take things less seriously at the moment and become more playful and spontaneous?
• Can you think of someone who might be described as an eternal child or a "big kid"?
• What is the danger of living in the past?
• What or who from your personal past can help shed some light on a present problem?

Keywords

Childhood, the past, a childlike nature, children, a blast from the past, reminiscence

Reversed: *Naivete, childishness, a difficult childhood, tantrums, living in the past*

7 of Cups

In the 7 of Cups we find a range of
options available. This card suggests
that many different opportunities or
paths are currently open to us. When
this happens, it is often difficult to
decide which to concentrate on and
which to dismiss.

In the main, the 7 of Cups suggests
a need for focus. When faced with a
handful of options, some of us ignore
them all, while others will try their
best to sample a little of each. When
we resist choosing any, we can easily
fall into the realm of daydreaming
about future plans, rather than actually
making them. Even when we try to
distribute our focus between many
options, there will eventually come a
time when we will need to attend to
one option over the others.

The 7 of Cups encourages us to
examine what opportunities are on offer and make a definite choice
between them.

7 of Cups as a Situation

Sometimes, opportunities can be like buses: you wait around for what seems like
ages and then a handful come along at the same time. With so much choice on
offer, making the right decision is not easy. The 7 of Cups could arise when we
have more than one career option to choose from. Maybe you recently attended
a selection of different job interviews, and now you must choose which job
would be best for you at this time. Similar situations could materialize in our
love lives, leaving us confused about which potential partner is right to date
right now.

The problem with opportunities is that they might not last forever. The
options hinted at by the 7 of Cups could well diminish as quickly as they

arrive, so a decision really needs to be made promptly. While you mustn't rush important decisions, it's worth remembering that if you leave a choice for too long, it may not still be available in the morning.

7 of Cups as a Person

Due to a lack of real focus, the person described by the 7 of Cups is the daydreamer. This is the kind of person who spends time thinking about what they are going to do, rather than actually getting around to doing it. Of course, this makes them a very imaginative person who can see the world through a variety of different lenses, but if you are looking for someone who will just roll their sleeves up and get the job done, you might need to look elsewhere.

The person with a 7 of Cups personality will usually have many ideas and projects on the back-burner. They might start a job but will become distracted and move on to another relatively quickly. Their enthusiasm for all of their projects won't fade, but with so many to concentrate on, they will be unable to give any single one their full attention.

7 of Cups and You

• Are you finding it difficult to choose just one option from a range of many possibilities?
• Have you fallen into daydreaming and fantasizing, rather than getting on with the job at hand?
• Can you think of someone who finds it difficult to stay focused on one thing?
• How could your time become more focused right now? What might you need to eliminate?

Keywords

Lack of focus, daydreams, options, a need for choice

Reversed: *Finding focus, setting intentions, making the right choice*

8 of Cups

In the 8 of Cups, we decide to move on. This is not an easy decision to make, though, since it means leaving stability and structure behind.

There will always be those times when we must edge out of our comfort zone. The 8 of Cups suggests that it's time to leave something behind because we no longer feel excited or challenged by it. While a relationship, job, or situation may have been satisfying and substantial for a good long time, the 8 of Cups can sometimes arise when we need more than has already been offered. Even though the road ahead is untested and could be beset with obstacles and challenges, this card reminds us that sometimes it's better to search for something new and inspiring than to stick with the tried and tested just because it is comfortable.

8 of Cups as a Situation

In personal relationships, the 8 of Cups can arise when it is time to move on. The problem with the 8 of Cups is that what is left is not necessarily bad. In fact, it is usually substantial and secure, but when this card turns up, it could be pointing out that something is missing and encourages us to consider what might be. Since this card is part of the suit of Cups, this move forward could be an emotional one. Not everyone is courageous enough to make the break, even if they feel the pull of a new mission.

In a career-oriented reading, the 8 of Cups could signify a desire to move on from a long-term job or to change career paths. We may feel that our needs have changed or that we need to spice things up a bit. For some, this will concern passing up their nine-to-five job and following a dream.

8 of Cups as a Person

In readings, the 8 of Cups is both exciting and challenging since it encourages us to connect with our spirit at the cost of security and established relationships. When the card describes a person, it can speak of someone who may consistently shirk responsibility, always chasing a new dream.

The 8 of Cups is not necessarily an unfavorable card because it asks us to think about those things we truly want, but when capturing the energy of a person, we could be looking at a traveler or someone who is consistently searching for something but is unable to find it. It is inspiring to go in search of ourselves and find those things we're destined to do and become, but this card could concern someone who is continually searching for the true love or dream job but is never satisfied.

8 of Cups and You

- What or who have you left behind in order to chase your dreams or become your authentic self?
- Can you think of someone who finds it hard to settle?
- What do you feel is missing in your life at the moment and how could you go about finding it?

Keywords

Moving on, abandoning something or someone, chasing a dream

Reversed: *Feeling stuck, unmotivated, lack of responsibility*

9 of Cups

Traditionally, the 9 of Cups is affectionately referred to as the "wish card." For many, if it comes up in a reading, it is confirmation of our wishes manifesting in reality.

The 9 of Cups reminds us that dreams are an important part of who we are. They provide us with hope and something to look forward to, and as we are all aware, some dreams do come true! This card brings our wishes to fruition and paves the way for personal joy and satisfaction.

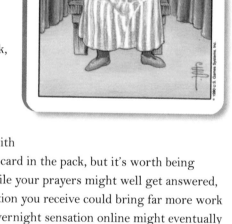

9 of Cups as a Situation

The 9 of Cups will arise to depict luck, abundance, and personal fulfillment. On a mundane level, things will fall into place and you might soon be feeling pretty pleased with your lot.

The 9 of Cups is in the running with the 4 of Wands for being the luckiest card in the pack, but it's worth being mindful about what you wish for. While your prayers might well get answered, this could come at a cost. The promotion you receive could bring far more work than you expected, or becoming an overnight sensation online might eventually become more of a hassle than it's worth.

9 of Cups as a Person

When the 9 of Cups arrives as a person in a reading, it can describe someone who appears to have it all. In some cases, they just might, since this card will present a character who appears to be knee-deep in their wildest dreams. There can, however, be a darker side to the personality displayed here. Like the cat that got the cream, this person can sometimes appear smug or self-centered.

It is important to remember that the joy experienced through the 9 of Cups is personal and received for the self alone. Those described by this card can often feel lonely beneath their bright and privileged exterior. In some cases, the inability to share their personal good fortune and joy is what eventually separates them from others.

9 of Cups and You

- If you could wish for something, what would be the first thing that comes to mind?
- What hidden cost was incurred from something you dreamed of and received?
- Do you know someone who appears to have it all? How do they make you feel?
- What is life without wishes and dreams?

Keywords

Wishes granted, personal satisfaction, abundance

Reversed: *Smugness, lack of belief, inability to share, greed*

10 of Cups

The 10 of Cups is a welcome card in most readings. For many, it represents a happy and emotionally fulfilling conclusion to all kinds of situations.

The 10 of Cups is often linked to family, and for this reason, signifies contentment and the luxury of heartfelt connection. Of course, this needn't represent only immediate relations: it can mirror relationships with close friends or anyone with whom we have a strong and significant emotional bond.

Contentment is often underrated. The 10 of Cups is not a promise of a certain lifestyle and financial abundance. Instead, it is about being satisfied with the life we already have and enjoying the people in it.

10 of Cups as a Situation

In many readings, people imagine that the 10 of Cups predicts a future they are yet to experience, and in the right positions in a layout, it will. It can, however, often ask us to think about those things and people in life that we are grateful for right now. Sometimes, we are so eager to believe that true fulfillment only exists in the future, that we do not realize what wonder we have in the present moment.

The 10 of Cups might suggest emotional stability and spending time with loved ones. When it turns up to depict a potential outcome, it can offer comfort and suggest that one will live "happily ever after." When looking into the future, it becomes a welcome sign.

It might not seem possible for a card like this to have a shadow side. For those who enjoy a challenge or have no intention of settling down just yet, the sweet conclusion suggested in this card might appear restrictive. As we have seen, however, one of the biggest problems with the 10 of Cups is whether we perceive it to be in our past, present, or future. Many will often recognize their own loving childhood, or crave an emotionally secure future environment, but fail to appreciate what is currently on offer to them.

10 of Cups as a Person

When the 10 of Cups materializes in a reading as person, it represents strength and security within love. In other cards you will find the initial flickers of attraction and even intense love affairs, but this card concerns everyday commitment and unconditional love. This card speaks of someone who has designs on a realistic future, rather than a fling or a fairytale.

Whether the person described has romantic intent or not, they will be emotionally committed. As well as being a lover or prospective life partner, the 10 of Cups could show up as a soul mate, lifelong friend, parent, or anyone who has your back in times of trouble. In terms of personality, they will be emotionally receptive and consistent. This is most definitely someone you can trust.

10 of Cups and You

- Can you think of a 10 of Cups moment in your life, when you have felt contented and fulfilled with your life?
- How do the meanings associated with the 10 of Cups mirror your life at t his time?
- Can you think of someone who is secure and happy with their place in the world, regardless of whether they have an abundance of money or success?
- What does "emotional wealth" look like to you?

Keywords

Contentment, fulfillment, happiness, unconditional love

Reversed: *Feeling discontented, fear of commitment, unrealistic goals*

Page of Cups

The Page of Cups is the most sensitive of the tarot youngsters. They have an open heart, which they are willing to share with those around them.

The Page of Cups will fall in love easily. Because they are connected to the element of Water, they experience their environment through their emotions and feelings. The problems of the physical world can create a huge weight on their small shoulders, and they can be hurt easily. Their biggest desire is to share their love, and they might wonder why everyone else is not so quick to do the same.

Page of Cups as a Person

Despite wanting to give love, they are also hungry to receive it. While they possess a great deal of natural empathy and compassion, they can sometimes become overwhelmed by the intensity and mechanics of mature relationships because of their naivete. Due to their lack of experience, they can come across as needy or even obsessive when involved with a romantic partner. They may believe they have enough love for both people in the relationship, which might feel smothering.

At best, the Page of Cups is a warm and enthusiastic friend or lover. They are both thoughtful and caring, always thinking of ways in which they can express their feelings—whether through art, poetry, love notes, or a good-night message. They have a strong connection to both their own intuition and the emotions of others, allowing them to accurately tap into how people are feeling and offer some carefully chosen words of comfort.

Page of Cups as a Situation

As a situation, the Page of Cups can speak of the new and exciting beginnings of something we are emotionally invested in. On a romantic level, this could be the start of a relationship and the butterflies we get in our stomach when we are getting to know someone new. In some cases, it may suggest our own abundant feelings or the enthusiasm of a partner.

All of the tarot Pages are learning to live within their element. Even though the Page of Cups can show up as a youth, it doesn't mean that the cards cannot describe someone older. Regardless of our age, we are not all emotionally mature. We've all heard the expression "there's no fool like an old fool"—this card can highlight the foolhardy in all of us. While starting new relationships can and should be exciting, the card might act as a caution—are we sharing our feelings too quickly or becoming so blinded by our emotions that we ignore the realities and practicalities of a situation?

When someone has been through a difficult time, the Page of Cups can suggest learning to trust again. If you have closed your heart because of previous relationship problems, this card could describe learning to open it slowly, in the hope of finding love again.

The Page of Cups can bring news of an emotional nature. Love letters, romantic invitations, and the news of a birth are likely.

Page of Cups and You

• Can you remember the first days of a new romantic relationship and how they felt?
• Do you open your heart to others too easily or do you hold back your feelings?
• What does the phrase "There's no fool like an old fool" mean to you?
• How in touch are you with your intuition and feelings?

Keywords

Sensitive, emotional, intuitive, psychic ability, an open heart

Reversed: *Self-absorbed, emotionally immature, untrusting, moody*

Knight of Cups

Like all of the tarot Knights, the Knight of Cups is on the move, and he (though the knight can represent a female) is in pursuit of his chosen goal. Since this young man is connected to the element of Water and emotion, he is usually depicted as someone in search of love.

Knight of Cups as a Person

All of the Knights are motivated by their element and focused on their desires. In the case of the Knight of Cups, we find someone who is stirred by how he feels inside. With an enthusiastic heart, he doesn't only search for a partner; with high expectations, he pins his heart on the one true and perfect love.

The Knight of Cups will often turn up as a lover in readings. The gender of this card is less important than his intention, since this Knight can describe anyone who wishes to commit emotionally to another person, however realistic this might be.

While the Knight of Cups is an obvious symbol to seek out in romantic readings, he could symbolize our connection to anyone in which we have an emotional investment. If he shows up as a person in your life, he will advise that you are loved and cared about.

In a challenging position, the Knight of Cups can neglect other aspects of life. He can become so involved with his feelings that he may lack practical skills or forget to think things through.

Knight of Cups as a Situation

All Knights are associated with movement. The Knight of Cups is steadier and more careful in his movement than some of his tarot cousins (notably the Knight of Wands and the Knight of Swords), but his motivation is as strong. He could indicate an emotional journey or romantic weekend away. Any trip that is based around the emotions, such as a pilgrimage, could be suggested when this card is in play.

For some of us, the card will describe our search for a lover. At best, this card can describe our pursuit of a relationship or even someone who is interested in developing a union with us, but we must remember to be realistic in our search. If the vision in your mind does not match the person in reality, you may feel disappointed and let down by your expectations.

At worst, the Knight of Cups can become manipulative. In a challenging or reversed position, we might find someone who plays with our emotions or isn't trustworthy.

Knight of Cups and You

- Are you planning a romantic holiday or have you received an invitation of an emotional nature?
- Could the Knight of Cups hint at someone who has an emotional interest in you?
- Do you need to reveal your emotions or romantic intent to another person at this time?
- Does a new lover appear "too good to be true"?

Keywords

Romantic, lover, emotional invitation, proposal, romantic trip

Reversed: *Unrealistic expectations, manipulative, obsessive lover, romantic problems*

Queen of Cups

The Queen of Cups rules the element of Water and is at one with the realm of emotions. Her feelings are the language with which she has learned to communicate, and many turn to her when in need of emotional support.

Queen of Cups as a Person

There is gentleness to the Queen of Cups. Being compassionate and receptive to the needs of others, she makes a worthy friend and confidant. If we wish to share our problems with a person who cares, there will always be time in this Queen's schedule for us to offload our worries. She is a good listener and can impart well-meaning advice. In fact, she is so naturally sensitive that she can often be found in a caring profession or in relationship guidance, where she can offer her heartfelt wisdom to clients.

The Queen of Cups is the most intuitive of the four Queens. Not only is she able to check in with her own feelings, she is also very good at tapping into those of others. Many suggest that she, like all of the Court of Cups, has psychic skills. She is, indeed, a very spiritual woman and can use her sensitivity for clairvoyance and clairaudience. She may work as a medium or tarot reader, or within some other means of spiritual counseling.

Although the Queen of Cups can touch the hidden realms with ease, she finds it difficult to function within the material world. Some may accuse her of being out of touch with reality, and they have a point. This Queen can be so immersed within her emotions or the emotional lives of others that day-to-day practicalities, such as paying the bills or keeping on top of her physical well-being, can easily get neglected.

Queen of Cups as a Situation

As a nurturer, the Queen of Cups can symbolize a time when we need to reflect on our emotions. Not everyone is comfortable with this or knows exactly how to do it, so the card could suggest enlisting some help. This could be in the form of a trusted friend, a therapist, or even a spiritual professional. Booking a reading, seeing a trained advisor, or going to see a friend for a chat could do wonders and helps us to emotionally unwind.

In a reading, the Queen of Cups can advise us to act as she does. If we have been worrying about something or are unsure of which avenue to take next, she might be asking us to lean on our intuition rather than rationality. The Queen of Cups asks how we feel about a situation. Have you ever had a strong feeling about someone, but couldn't explain why, only to be proved right at a later date? The Queen of Cups encourages us to take notice of how we feel, rather than base our opinion only on what we can see and *think* we know.

Queen of Cups and You

- How in touch are you with your emotions?
- When was the last time you trusted your gut feeling and were proved right?
- Can you think of someone, like the Queen of Cups, who is a caring friend and good listener?
- Is your emotional life in balance with your physical life?

Keywords

Empathic, emotional, sensitive, caring, psychic

Reversed: *Unrealistic, overemotional, self-absorbed, out of touch with emotions*

King of Cups

The King of Cups is in touch with his emotions. He is strong and compassionate, happy to use his own empathy and emotional experience to help others during times of difficulty.

King of Cups as a Person

All of the members of the Cups family are motivated by the element of Water and their emotions, but unlike the younger members of his clan, and even his consort, the King of Cups is not ruled by his feelings. In fact, he understands how to control them. This can help him to be an effective counselor or advisor, since he knows how to master his deepest feelings, even when the world seems to be falling apart around him. In a professional role, this person guides others through their emotional experiences with ease and maturity, able to sympathize through personal experience but also to proactively help point them in the direction of recovery and self-understanding.

As a lover, the King of Cups is caring and understanding. This is someone who is stable and will listen to your thoughts and feelings. If he has a fault, it might be that some of his partners may find him cold. Since he is in complete control of his own ideas and reactions, he can occasionally appear aloof or as though he is holding back his true feelings.

In a challenging position, the King of Cups can be manipulative. He understands how others work so well that it allows him to con or scam. His empathy and understanding could well be a guise, constructed to get what he wants from us. When reversed, this card presents a warning and asks who we can really trust.

King of Cups as a Situation

Are you currently involved in a situation or relationship that is affecting you emotionally? The King of Cups could be suggesting that you try to detach from your feelings and approach things from a rational and logical viewpoint. This is not always easy. When dealing with the emotions of someone else, however, it could be vital to maintain a mature and practical involvement. Others may depend on your strength to cope when they cannot.

The King of Cups can suggest emotional maturation but might easily arise as a confident and compassionate advisor. Due to the way the cards rank within the Court system, this king is likely to be someone who helps you from a professional perspective (such as a therapist, counselor, or doctor), rather than the friendly ear of someone who cares. While they are experienced within the world of personal relationships and emotions, they do not allow these things to cloud their view or control their heart.

King of Cups and You

- Who do you turn to for support when the going gets tough?
- How important is it to detach from your heart during an emotional situation?
- How might someone like this King, who is emotionally understanding and compassionate, become manipulative?
- Can you think of a time when holding back how you are feeling could be detrimental or appear cold and uncaring to others?

Keywords

Loving, supportive, empathic, in control of his feelings, counselor

Reversed: *Manipulative, untrustworthy, cold, antisocial, not a "people person"*

SWORDS

Ace of Swords

Like all of the Aces, the Ace of Swords can be viewed as a seed. Within the element of Air, this is one of new thoughts and ideas.

A single Sword can be used to cut through doubt or confusion, so this card is often concerned with a new understanding and clarity. It can present itself as a brainwave, an aha moment, or as the ability to see something clearly for the first time.

When this card comes up in a reading, it can represent a new idea we might have had. In itself, the idea might be relatively small, but with nurture and consideration, it can become the basis of something far bigger. All of the greatest books, inventions, and technology started with just a simple idea.

Ace of Swords as a Situation

The suit of Swords can sometimes, fairly or unfairly, become linked to strife. It is, however, often during more difficult times that a new idea or potential solution is beneficial and will instigate change. Because Swords can cut to the heart of a situation, this card will often appear at its most powerful when finding a solution to a problem or clarifying something which had previously eluded us.

Many people see the Ace of Swords as being like a light bulb switching on above their heads, so the card might arrive in a reading to confirm that a new way of doing something is, in fact, worthy of pursuing. In a legal situation, the card might allude to the truth being uncovered or the inclusion of important information that will enhance the case.

Ace of Swords as a Person

The person described by the Ace of Swords will have a fertile imagination. They might not be a deep thinker, but their mind will be an incubator for imaginative and bright ideas. This is someone who enjoys thinking up new ways of doing things and finding potential solutions to problems.

As well as being connected to our thoughts, Swords relate to communication as well. Voicing the truth in as clear and accurate a way as possible is of the highest importance to someone represented by the Ace of Swords.

ACE of SWORDS.

Ace of Swords and You

- Can you remember a small idea that manifested big change in your life?
- What might help you to see a situation more clearly?
- What truth do you need to voice at this time?
- How might a potentially difficult situation become the breeding ground for a new and innovative idea?

Keywords

Ideas, thoughts, clarity, communication, truth, being smart

Reversed: *Confusion, doubt, lack of understanding, lies*

2 of Swords

Within traditional tarot, a single sword represents an idea, but what happens when we are presented with two? Each of the two swords might offer an interesting or credible perspective, but which is the right one to choose?

The 2 of Swords can deliver the idea of choice in a reading, but the problem we face is in which option to take. When we are indecisive and choose neither, we are unable to move forward.

2 of Swords as a Situation

Naturally, most of us have experienced a 2 of Swords moment more than once. Quite often, a choice will be involved. As an example, we may be required to choose between two college courses, two lovers, or the best way to approach a problem. Have you ever been in a situation where both options seemed equally appealing and you could not decide which to choose for the best?

When this card arrives in a reading, things could be at a standstill. This might concern an inner conflict, or it may even represent the locked swords of the subject of the reading and an opponent. If the card is suggesting an argument or stalemate, the 2 of Swords confirms that neither party is likely to budge anytime soon. Therefore, we will need to use our common sense to work out what the most beneficial step forward should be. The suit of Swords is one of the rational mind. In most cases, this will be the best tool for the job but when we can no longer find *our way* to a solution, it could suggest seeking the unbiased perspective of a third party for advice if we want to make some headway.

2 of Swords as a Person

As a person, the 2 of Swords will represent the indecisive among us. When a person is described by this card, they will find life's decisions to be huge and weighty, regardless of whether they are life-changing or mundane. Being a person of thought, they will overanalyze their options and tick off the pros and cons of every potential possibility. While this is not a bad thing to do sometimes, they might do better to make a move based on what they know already.

The person described by the 2 of Swords can often become disconnected from their heart and emotions. This will often show someone in denial or who wishes to bury their feelings concerning a specific situation. Because of this, they might find it increasingly difficult to move on from trauma and find healing.

2 of Swords and You

• Are you using your heart or head when faced with a decision?
• What might you be avoiding at this time?
• Can you think of a present choice that needs to be made? How would life be better if you made it today?
• How could you use compassion to move forward with someone you're in conflict with at this time?

Keywords

Choice, avoiding decisions, denial, stalemate

Reversed: *Taking action, a decision is taken out of your hands, facing problems*

3 of Swords

While cards from the suit of Swords involve thoughts and communication, their appearance in a reading can sometimes be troublesome. One of the cards traditionally associated with pain and difficulty is the 3 of Swords.

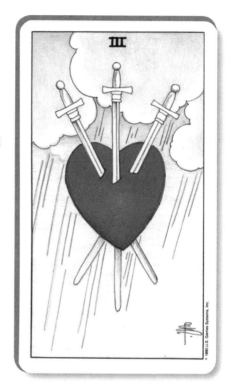

The 3 of Swords is often connected to heartbreak and upset. In some readings, this will be relevant to a relationship breakup or argument, but it could suggest pain that is lingering from our past. Although we think of a wounded heart as a testament of hurt feelings, the effects of the 3 of Swords can also taint our minds as well.

In all tarot cards, whether positive or negative, there is always room for insight and growth. When harsh words or an indiscretion pierces our heart, do we allow it to fester and poison, or do we try our best to repair the damage and learn from the bad experience? The 3 of Swords might feel unjust and bitterly unkind in a reading, but with it comes some responsibility. Do we allow our experiences to control us or do we take a first step toward healing?

3 of Swords as a Situation

Although the suit of Swords primarily relates to the mind, the 3 of Swords will appear when our heart is broken and our feelings have been stamped upon. In that sense, it will arise to suggest the breakdown or breakup of a romance. In some cases, the third sword may suggest the involvement of a third person within a relationship issue.

If the 3 of Swords arises within a nonromantic reading, then it can describe petty arguments and disputes. While these may not have a major influence on a situation, they could incur temporary separation, or time apart for both parties to lick their wounds.

3 of Swords as a Person

As a person, the 3 of Swords will describe someone who is hurting. This person might be experiencing deep pain from a past separation and they may feel unable to leave it behind. In some cases, the first step to doing so could be through forgiveness, which might prevent the subject from carrying their pain any longer. However, there may be some people who are unwilling to release the hurt. This card represents those who find moving on a difficult hurdle to confront, but there will be others who consciously dwell within the darker aspects of life and experience.

When signifying a person in a reading, the 3 of Swords could speak of someone who is stuck within deep grief. This person will be profoundly affected by the loss of a loved one and may be unable to move on. Should this be the person sitting for a reading, it is recommended that you guide them toward a professional who is experienced in dealing with grief.

3 of Swords and You

- Can you remember a time when an argument hurt your feelings or led to a parting of the ways?
- How have you learned to heal after significant grief or a breakup?
- Can you think of someone who dwells within the difficult aspects of their experiences and shows little interest in moving forward?
- How could forgiveness help release you from something that happened in your own past?

Keywords

Heartbreak, grief, arguments, relationship breakdown

Reversed: *Healing, avoiding problems, forgiveness*

4 of Swords

If we are to perform at our very best, a little time-out every so often is a necessity. The 4 of Swords is a card of much-needed rest and recuperation— not just of the body but the mind as well.

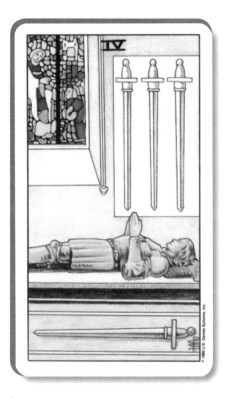

Most of us lead hectic lives these days. As well as nurturing our families, friendships, and careers, many people have the added pressures of social media and a variety of hobbies and groups to keep up with. Of course, running from one place to another can take its toll and leave us physically fatigued. A good night's sleep can often rectify this, but it is not always so easy to pacify our overactive thoughts or worries. The 4 of Swords can act as a warning suggesting that this is exactly what we need to try to do.

4 of Swords as a Situation

The 4 of Swords will sometimes turn up after we have been through an ordeal, and it will encourage us to take a break. If a relationship has broken down, the card is asking us to step back and take some time to breathe. If we've been through a period of ill health, or even an operation, then we're being encouraged to recuperate and allow recovery to weave its magic.

Since the suit of Swords is connected to the mind, this card often suggests that a calming of our thoughts is needed. This might concern a little quiet time or even a session of meditation.

4 of Swords as a Person

The person described by the 4 of Swords may be viewed as quiet and gentle. The card could speak of someone who knows how to control their thoughts. This person knows when silence is a greater strength than aggression, especially when in their pursuit of the truth. In our general day-to-day life, this card can represent those people who are chilled out and calm in a crisis.

In challenging situations, the restful nature of the 4 of Swords could become a problem. It can speak of someone who doesn't stand up for themselves or is even lazy. There will be times when a lack of reaction to important events can become frustrating. The person may be so "chilled out" that they are literally horizontal.

4 of Swords and You

• How much do you need a break or holiday at this time?
• What do you think will be the result of physically or emotionally overworking yourself right now?
• How can you begin to ease your mind of toxic or worrying thoughts?
• Who is the most relaxed and chilled-out person you know? What is their secret to not letting life get on top of them?

Keywords

Rest, recuperation, meditation, a period of calm

Reversed: *Overworking, overthinking, ignoring the signs of needed rest, laziness*

5 of Swords

We all encounter conflict from time to time. In our modern world, it's pretty much impossible to avoid, whether it crops up within an established relationship or with an acquaintance. The 5 of Swords brings about petty arguments, major disputes, and all that lies in between.

The 5 of Swords is a card of battle, but rather than a balanced and healthy fight, it often presents the aggressive defeat of one party. Inevitably, disputes usually claim a winner and a loser. If we're the loser, then this will be a time of disappointment. If we win the fight, our accomplishment may feel hollow, as using aggression to undermine an opponent may leave a sour taste in one's mouth.

5 of Swords as a Situation

At its most positive, the 5 of Swords will describe those times when we stand up for ourselves and win. It might suggest a complaint made and acknowledged, or a situation where it is imperative that we keep pushing to the bitter end. Most people, however, approach this card from the other side. The 5 of Swords often manifests as a roadblock that cannot be passed, regardless of how hard we try.

While admitting defeat may not be the preferred option for many, it can sometimes show strength. When an opponent is too big to take on and we know we are unable to win the fight, is it not better to walk away with self-respect than to take another hit? Although this card can indicate strife within personal relationships, we will also find it representing fights with the government, employers, or any kind of establishment that has a wider set of resources than our own.

5 of Swords as a Person

As a person, we find someone of strength. Due to the negative connotations of this card, they might appear ruthless and unemotional in their dealings.

The person described by the 5 of Swords can often be argumentative; in some cases, this might appear to be for the sake of it. As someone who enjoys winning at whatever cost, they will resort to low blows or intentionally try to hurt others.

We all come up against a person like this at some point, but this card asks us to choose our battles carefully. Is it really worth reacting to their invitation to fight, or would it be better to smile and bow out with dignity?

5 of Swords and You

• Can you tell when a fight is worth participating in or not?
• What does the term "hollow victory" mean to you?
• Can you remember a time when you'd have been better off to have walked away from conflict or a dispute?
• Can you remember a time when you won an argument at the expense of somebody else's feelings?

Keywords

Defeat, loss, battle, conflict

Reversed: *Holding on to resentment, walking away from conflict*

6 of Swords

The 6 of Swords is a card of transition.
While it can sometimes represent
a physical journey, it is most often
associated with a journey of the mind.
The difficulties in life can often be
viewed as teachers, and this card is
an acknowledgement of those things
we have learned during the process of
hardship.

Traditionally, this card concerns
moving on from a disruptive situation
toward a place of healing. For many
people, the 6 of Swords offers quieter
horizons and a time to reflect on those
things that may have been problematic.
If we are in the middle of strife, then
this card suggests that things will
begin to get better. However, it is
also encouraging us to take the first
step toward a safer place by removing
ourselves from toxic people and drama.

6 of Swords as a Situation

The 6 of Swords is asking us to overrule our emotions with fact. It is so easy
to become overwhelmed by emotional issues, and the 6 of Swords suggests we
find some focus and clarity. In many cases, we should take ourselves out of a
situation so that it can be seen from a distance.

Traditionally, the 6 of Swords can become the instigator of trips, especially
those over water. Taking a break—whether it be a weekend away or even a
holiday—might be a good way of beginning to clear the mind after trauma.

As well as concerning physical trips, the 6 of Swords could suggest a
journey of the mind. When this card is present in a reading, it could hint at
new ways of looking at something, or perhaps a release of anger and regret.
The transition suggested may concern a complete overhaul of beliefs and

values. Anyone who has turned their life around for the better by leaving disruptive relationships or influences behind will recognize their own personal journey in this card.

6 of Swords as a Person

It is likely that the person described by this card has been through a period of suffering. With this in mind, they might support others through a similar transition, as a sponsor.

As a person, the 6 of Swords is a calming influence, which can emotionally ferry us from a place of distress to somewhere where we can breathe comfortably once again. This card could indicate a friend, counselor, or even a buddying-up program that allows us to work through our problems from a safe distance.

Due to its connection to travel, the 6 of Swords will describe travelers of all means. It might concern those working within the tourism industry or a backpacker off to see the world.

6 of Swords and You

• How can you release yourself from toxic people and difficult situations at this time?
• Are there prospects for physical travel in your life at the moment?
• Can you think of someone who has helped guide you through the troubled waters of a tense situation?
• How can you help someone who is currently dealing with stress or conflict?

Keywords

Transition, healing, travel, overcoming emotions with the mind

Reversed: *Staying within a difficult situation, being your own worst enemy, unable to keep your head above water*

7 of Swords

The 7 of Swords is a difficult card for many. While we'd all like to know if someone is being dishonest, and we might wish to flush out the cheat in our readings, this is not an easy card to turn. Like some of the other challenging cards within the tarot deck, it can provoke fear and anxiety in both the reader and seeker if not handled well.

The 7 of Swords does have a reputation for being underhanded, but in some situations, there may be good reason for this. People hide the truth for a multitude of reasons. While an unfaithful lover or sneaky businessperson may be uncovered by this card, it might also indicate news that has been kept secret to protect feelings.

7 of Swords as a Situation

The 7 of Swords is, of course, a card to keep an eye out for, since it can suggest that someone is covering up the truth. Though this might be for our own good, there will be times when the intention is to deceive and manipulate. The card might confirm a feeling we have had about a close friend or relative, but it might also indicate a need to check the small print in a business deal or be careful about an investment we are considering.

The 7 of Swords represents those who could be out to steal our ideas or are spying. Since these things are prevalent on the internet, the card could be telling us to adjust our settings or be careful about what information we share.

In its most positive light, the 7 of Swords will represent being assertive and one step ahead of others, such as hiding an early pregnancy or a surprise birthday party. If you have been secretly looking for a new job, it might be important to keep it to yourself until you have secured an offer.

7 of Swords as a Person

Of course, the 7 of Swords will describe a whole range of dishonest people. At its worst, it will pinpoint crooks or an adulterer, but, more likely, it will highlight those who tell "little white lies" or twist or exaggerate the truth to suit themselves.

In a positive light, the 7 of Swords describes someone who thinks outside the box and uses their intelligence to get ahead. It might describe a cunning person who needs to have their wits about them if the wish to succeed. In this sense, the card describes cleverness, independence, and a need to put yourself first. In some readings, this might be a skill that is vital for survival.

7 of Swords and You

• How honest are you with those around you?
• When is it acceptable to tell a little white lie?
• Can you think of a time when your trust was taken advantage of?
• When we think of theft, we think of stolen possessions. Can you think of other things that might be stolen?

Keywords

Deception, theft, a cunning person, selfishness, dishonesty

Reversed: *Dishonesty revealed, lies are out in the open, something that has been taken is found or returned*

8 of Swords

Thoughts can be used in so many inventive and creative ways, but the 8 of Swords is a reminder of how we can use them to confine and constrict our progress and imagination, rather than expand it. Sometimes, we can be our own worst enemy. Rather than boost our confidence, we doubt or discredit ourselves. It's easily done, and it can stop the strongest of us in our tracks.

When the 8 of Swords arrives in a reading, it presents an obstacle: however, the obstacle is not an external one. Instead, it is our own fears or lack of belief that hems us in and leaves us feeling trapped.

8 of Swords as a Situation

Some tarot readers might see the 8 of Swords as representing a physical situation that could imprison the subject of the reading. While there are likely instances where this could be true, the key to this card is realizing it's the mind that acts as the jailor, rather than the world around us. The 8 of Swords could turn up for someone who feels trapped within an unhealthy relationship. It sets out to remind us that it is our fear of walking away that holds us fast, rather than the other person.

As a situation, the 8 of Swords will describe occasions where we feel unable to move forward or speak our mind. Though we might know what's needed, we cannot always find the words or confidence to take action. Fear can become immobilizing. Past failures or the critical views of others could lead us to believe that we don't have what it takes, but this card suggests we simply need a shift of perspective to free ourselves from bondage.

8 of Swords as a Person

As a person, the 8 of Swords will speak of someone who feels restricted. In some cases, it will represent a person who is physically restrained. This might be through incarceration, but it could also describe a person who is bedridden, physically handicapped, unable to travel, or tied down by legal requirements or red tape.

Most often, the person described by the 8 of Swords will be restricted by their own thoughts. Therefore, we may find the card representing anyone who is fearful, shy, or too nervous to express themselves properly. In some cases, this will be more profound and could describe someone with low self-confidence or destructive thoughts.

8 of Swords and You

• How does insecurity prevent you from moving forward?
• In what area of life do you feel restricted?
• What thoughts or self-criticisms are hindering your progress?
• What boundaries have been imposed on you, by either yourself or others?

Keywords

Feeling trapped, restriction, mental block, insecurity, limited thinking

Reversed: *Moving toward freedom, free thought, release*

9 of Swords

Have you ever woken up in the middle of the night overwhelmed by worry? Maybe you'd awoken from a nightmare, or perhaps a very real problem had followed you into the twilight hours. Whether fear hits at night or during the light of day, the 9 of Swords represents those times when we are held captive by worry and anxiety.

Most often, the things we worry about come to nothing. We can spend hours agonizing over something that may never happen. We might worry that our partner will be unfaithful, that we are seriously ill, or that we'll never have enough money to pay off our debts. While it is true that worry does nothing to aid a problem and that the majority of our fears are unlikely to actually manifest, worrying can result in very real panic attacks or sleepless nights.

What we must remember when the 9 of Swords is drawn is that our worries are no more than thoughts. And, in reality, thoughts should not be able to hurt us. When we begin to worry unnecessarily (and it will be unnecessarily if this card is drawn), we should remember the acronym FEAR—False Evidence Appearing Real. Unless fact tells us there really is something to become anxious about, there is little point becoming lost within the fiction of needless worry.

9 of Swords as a Situation

At its heart, the 9 of Swords suggests that a scenario has become inflamed by worry. Of course, this could hint at a situation you are fearful of. Maybe a driving test or results from the doctor are on the horizon. Maybe we are scared for the well-being of someone else. Much of the time, we will be adding two to two and getting five, since fearful emotions can dramatically overrule the mind.

The 9 of Swords can be a lonely card, and as we know, when we have something on our mind, we can feel very much alone in our worries—even if we have close friends or family around us. In a situation, this card advises us to speak to someone about our fears. Often, the best way of cutting a worry down to size is by saying it aloud, which can exercise its power over you. Tell someone you trust about what scares you and see if that doesn't begin to reduce your fear.

9 of Swords as a Person

As a person, the 9 of Swords can represent someone who is suffering from anxiety. Since some of us can successfully hide our emotions from others (and even ourselves), the card may uncover a deep-rooted fear that a person has buried well. Stress is a very real problem, and it can affect a person's emotional, mental, and physical health. This card could represent the first step in dealing with fear-based problems.

At its most challenging, the 9 of Swords is a worrywart—someone who is naturally pessimistic and who will worry regularly and unnecessarily. While we should usually take the concerns of others seriously, there will always be some person who is consistently consumed by worry. They will be unable to tell the difference between a drama and a crisis, feeding both with the same amount of fear.

9 of Swords and You
• What worry, if any, is keeping you awake at night?
• How real are your worries?
• Can you remember a worry that ended up as being totally unnecessary?
• Who do you trust enough to share your concerns with?

Keywords
Worry, anxiety, fear, nightmares, sleepless nights

Reversed: *Depression, overcoming fear, accepting help*

10 of Swords

Like a handful of the cards from its
suit, the 10 of Swords is notoriously
challenging. Many traditionalists see
it as the darkest hour before dawn,
suggesting a difficult and sometimes
painful ending to a situation. It is one
of the less welcome cards in the tarot,
but if the cards are to mirror life's ups
and downs, it's important that both
light and dark aspects are included.

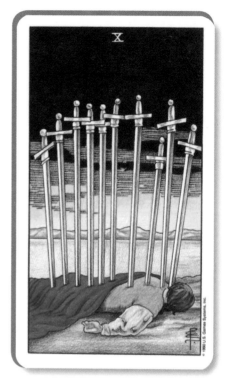

Unfortunately, not everything
works out as we'd like it to. While
some relationships will end amicably
and some people will ascend
effortlessly through their career, there
will be many of us who experience
bad breakups or failure, or who end
up feeling as though the world has
chewed us up and spit us out. The
10 of Swords will highlight the pain
endured by a difficult situation, but believe
me, it won't kill you. In fact, it will probably make you stronger in the long run.

Even though the 10 of Swords is not a card most readers like to see in a
reading, there is a light at the end of its tunnel. However painful an ending is
likely to be, we know that it will soon be over.

10 of Swords as a Situation

When the 10 of Swords arrives in a reading, it depicts the final sword in the
back of a situation—the last blow. There is no denying the stress and upset
involved with a transition like this, but it will be necessary. For some, seeing
this card on the table will be confirmation of the pain they are experiencing,
which can actually be a relief, because it suggests that things can't get
any worse.

The 10 of Swords can indicate the culmination of arguments, strife, or bad choices. It may suggest the messy breakdown of a relationship or the wounds of a public embarrassment. But whatever it is, you know that you will live to see another day. The reason that some see this as the darkest hour before dawn is that a new day of fresh possibility will surely follow.

10 of Swords as a Person

As a person, the 10 of Swords depicts someone who is at their lowest point: they'll feel exhausted and may well have lost the inclination to carry on fighting. It is highly likely that we will see these signs when a loved one is suffering mental or emotional decline; this card could be warning for us to step in and help before they hit rock bottom.

When someone is described by the 10 of Swords, the only way is up. Despite the sympathy we might feel for a person in this situation, some responsibility is required on their part. Many will see this stage in their life as something to build from, and they will learn from the experience, however harrowing. Of course, there will always be the odd soul who doesn't try to help themselves and will dwell in this stage for longer than is needed.

10 of Swords and You

• Can you think back to a difficult ending that is now well and truly behind you?
• How painful does a situation need to get before you ask for help?
• How might the 10 of Swords be useful to someone currently experiencing pain?
• What might be the danger of dwelling on a difficult situation?

Keywords

Difficult endings, pain, suffering, feeling betrayed or stabbed in the back

Reversed: *Releasing pain, moving forward, avoiding recovery*

Page of Swords

The Page of Swords bursts with ideas. He or she is a creature of the mind, always thinking and always curious.

Natural curiosity can often be seen within young children. They want to know what everything is, how things work, and why they exist. They will ask question after question, their curious mind continually eager for more information. You can almost hear their brains ticking away, preparing their next question or mulling over a new idea. The Page of Swords rests within all curious minds; they enjoy thinking up new solutions and are enthusiastic about finding the truth within any situation.

Page of Swords as a Person

While the gathering of information can be necessary, there will be times when natural curiosity becomes out of balance, and in tarot tradition, the Page of Swords has often been referred to as sneaky in their pursuit of the truth. When in a challenging position, they may become underhanded in their methods for finding out the facts, their actions bordering on spying or stalking for information. This is the kind of person who will obtain what they need at any cost.

Page of Swords as a Situation

We all exhibit the characteristics of the Page of Swords on occasion. There will be times when we wish to eradicate doubt or find a fresh way of dealing with an old problem. When the Page of Swords shows up in a reading, they can speak of seeking knowledge and deepening our understanding of a particular subject. Their outlook might be youthful and lacking in experience, but it is sometimes that freshness that is required to go the extra mile; their childlike way of observing a situation shouldn't be overlooked too readily.

As with all of the Pages, the Page of Swords can be the bearer of messages within a reading. Due to being ruled by the element of Air, which is linked to thoughts and communication, they can predict verbal announcements and telephone calls. Information about travel plans may also be indicated.

It is important to remember that while you may crave information, not all news will be fortuitous and welcoming. The Page of Swords, when challenging, could provide difficult messages or alert us to someone with an unhealthy reliance on gossip.

Page of Swords and You

• How might a healthy curiosity aid you at this time?
• Do you have a new idea that it would be beneficial to follow up on?
• What are you interested in learning about at this time?
• How might curiosity and the seeking of truth become unhealthy or intrusive to others?

Keywords

Curiosity, cleverness, sharp wit, talkative, ideas, announcement

Reversed: *Spying, gossipy, two-faced, confusion, challenging news*

Knight of Swords

The Knight of Swords is confident and assertive. Connected to the element of Air, he (though the knight can represent a female) is associated with both the mind and communication, making him an intelligent and naturally articulate ally or rival.

Knight of Swords as a Person

This Knight sees himself as a problem solver, and like all members of the Swords Court, *thinks* rather than *feels* his way through day-to-day life. Motivated by the truth, he believes that it is his job to pursue it and deliver it. Sometimes perceived as heroic, this young man doesn't think twice about forcing himself into a situation in order to try to untangle fact from fiction. Seeking justice is one of his inherent characteristics and highest ideals.

The Knight of Swords has many commendable attributes, since he is honest, sharp, and quick-witted. He can make an imaginative storyteller or a good researcher, but for some, his honesty may be a little difficult to handle. While his perception of a situation might be accurate, his delivery of the facts can occasionally be brutal or cutting. This Knight doesn't sugarcoat his words, because he is generally unaware that he needs to; this can leave the recipients of his sharp tongue feeling emotionally wounded and hurt.

At best, the Knight of Swords is someone to count on in a crisis. He can be a little heavy-handed at times, but his intention is pure. In short, he will fight on your behalf or for what he considers a worthy cause, working out the most effective way for you to get what he believes you deserve.

Knight of Swords as a Situation

All of the Knights are concerned with movement, and this Knight can describe or predict something that manifests at lightning speed. Due to his single-minded focus and ability to cut to the chase, the Knight of Swords can bring about great change within a reading. Due to the difficult nature of the Swords suit, these changes will be challenging, forcing you to react immediately and comply.

The Knight of Swords is probably the quickest of the four Knights. As a figure associated with the element of Air, this card might concern air travel or planning a flight.

Knight of Swords and You

- Is change always a bad thing?
- How might you use your communication skills in a positive manner?
- How might using humor defuse a difficult situation?
- Can you think of someone like this Knight, who engages his mouth before his brain?

Keywords

Conflict, sudden change, confident speaker, focused, travel by air

Reversed: *Abrupt, cutting, bossiness, cruelty, deceit*

Queen of Swords

The Queen of Swords is the thinking Queen. Rather than using her emotions to assess a situation, she relies on cold, hard facts. Connected with the element of Air and the mind, she chooses her words precisely and honestly.

We all need a friend like the Queen of Swords, because while she may be blunt at times, she is brave enough to be honest and doesn't shy away from the truth. Like all of the Queens, she can be both caring and loving. She speaks with confidence and clarity because she knows that she'd be doing her relationships a disservice by mollifying people instead of saying what needs to be said. Of course, there will be times when this will upset those around her. Not everyone is comfortable with being 100 percent honest with others; even fewer are eager to hear what someone really thinks about them.

Queen of Swords as a Person

The Queen of Swords is a nurturer of both her thoughts and what she says. On a professional level, you might find her within law, where facts are a necessity, or in a vocation where she might publicly speak or write. Because of her keenness to document the truth, you might find her working as a journalist or a police officer. If she is a friend or work colleague, then she is the woman (or man) you'd go to because you know she'll try her hardest to solve a problem and be fair.

When in a challenging position, the Queen of Swords can be prickly. If under attack, she will use her words and knowledge as weapons. She knows just which of our buttons to press and has no fear of pressing them. She can easily detach from her own emotions and when confronted will pull out all the stops to slice through someone else's feelings.

Queen of Swords as a Situation

As a nurturer of ideas, the Queen of Swords could be asking us to compile and organize information. This could be for an impending meeting, a court case, or a situation where factual information will be needed. This is a time where we must be precise and make sure that we have all of the relevant dates, times, and names needed. If this is not your forte, then the card could be asking that you enlist the help of a professional—maybe a secretary, proofreader, or caseworker.

As a situation, the Queen of Swords can suggest a time to be honest. We could be involved in a legal dispute, where we are required to tell the truth, but in a personal relationship, it might be time to tell a friend or partner how we really feel. For many, this is never an easy thing to do. The Queen of Swords is asking that we first be honest with ourselves, and if we have been avoiding something or have allowed others to believe a story that isn't wholly true, then this card suggests we provide them with the facts.

Queen of Swords and You

• Are you comfortable with being honest with others?
• Can you think of someone like the Queen of Swords, whom you admire for being true to her own opinion?
• How honest are you with yourself?
• Can you think of an area in your life where an emotional response is less important than a rational one?

Keywords

Honest, opinionated, knowledgeable, an independent thinker

Reversed: *Insensitive, vindictive, liar, manipulative*

King of Swords

The King of Swords is a master of the mind. His perception is razor sharp and he has a clear idea of what is right and wrong. As a creature of communication, this man is comfortable giving fair judgements and making rational decisions.

Knight of Swords as a Person

Like all of the members of the Swords Court, this King is someone who favors factual evidence. Since he sits at the top of the pile, his experience allows him to accurately determine the truth in a situation. Therefore, we will often find him in positions of authority, where the truth must be upheld, such as in law. He might arise in a reading as a judge or high-ranking police officer.

KING of SWORDS.

The King of Swords enjoys deciphering puzzles and finding solutions to problems. If he is a friend or advisor, then having him around will be to our benefit; his need for clarity and transparency is second to none, and he'll do all he can to defend what he believes to be just.

As a lover, this king could symbolize a mature partner. We might enjoy picking his brain or letting him recount his experiences, since his knowledge and power can be extremely seductive. While this can start out as both interesting and exciting, this king can become judgemental in a relationship and sometimes appear coldhearted. At worst, we may feel as though our words and actions are being examined or criticized. With a silver tongue, this man has the ability to lift our spirits, but he can just as easily crush us with a few well-chosen words.

King of Swords as a Situation

As a situation, the King of Swords suggests a need for fairness and accuracy. We might be encouraged to make an important choice, based on factual evidence rather than opinion or emotional ties. The King of Swords does not rely on emotion, and there must be no gray area within the process of making a decision. This man is a figure of justice and finding this card in a reading suggests that we need to behave rationally, rather than act from the heart.

If we feel unable to think logically or choose the best road forward without emotional attachment, then this card could be suggesting that we find someone who can. Whether they are an advisor, spokesperson, or legal representative, they will be able to see a situation for what it really is. Although the King of Swords often works within a professional capacity, he can arrive in a reading as a fair parent, friend, or clearheaded individual willing to help.

King of Swords and You

- How difficult is it for you to be rational within a personal or emotionally charged situation?
- Can you think of someone you'd go to now, personally or professionally, who would give you advice, unhindered by opinion or bias?
- How might another person hurt you with the truth?
- Can you remember a time when you defended someone who you believed to be telling the truth?

Keywords

Intelligent, authoritative, fair, honest, analytical, accurate

Reversed: *Unfair, exploitative, cruel, judgemental, legal issues*

PENTACLES

Ace of Pentacles

The Ace of Pentacles is welcome in just about every kind of reading. It represents a gift from the Earth, often manifesting as an opportunity or some kind of physical boost.

Because the suit of Pentacles deals with finances and monetary concerns, many see the Ace as being a sure sign of money and wealth. Of course, there will be times when the card does predict a bonus or a little unexpected cash, but it isn't as likely to bring a windfall as some readers might believe. In fact, due to being the first card in the suit, it could provide a leg-up in business rather than solve all of our economic problems.

If we have been experiencing financial difficulties, then the Ace of Pentacles will symbolize an opportunity worth taking. This might be a slim handout or a way of helping us to get back on our feet. This might not sound particularly exciting, but this is not a card to be sniffed at. It carries the potential for great reward in the long run. Any real benefit will still need to be worked for, though.

Ace of Pentacles as a Situation

As a situation, the Ace of Pentacles could suggest a financial boost. While this could be a gift or small inheritance, it may even manifest as money owed. It might not answer all our prayers at a single stroke, but a small cash injection could provide the means to make more money down the line. A business loan, an investment in one's talents, or an advance of a paycheck are ways in which the Ace of Pentacles could help us get on our feet financially.

Due to the physical nature of this card, the Ace of Pentacles might suggest a job offer on the horizon. The road ahead may still contain occasional twists and turns, but the Ace of Pentacles symbolizes that first rung on the ladder to success. The rest, of course, depends on us.

In a romantic reading, this card could represent commitment. A partner may be offering a stable future, should their proposal be accepted. The Ace of Pentacles can also alert us to someone who thinks we are worth their time.

Ace of Pentacles as a Person

All of the Aces are symbolic of new beginnings and each holds the potential for great things. In that sense, the Ace of Pentacles represents someone who is likely to have a promising future. This may well be down to a good work ethic and the ability to get sucked into a project or job.

The person described by the Ace of Pentacles will have vision. Within the smallest of projects or situations, they will be able to see what could become a reality. These visions are not pipe dreams, though; they are projected outcomes built from very real expectations. This person has the potential of great strength and determination within them.

Ace of Pentacles and You
• Can you think of a time where a small investment garnered a large reward?
• How might you use a little extra cash at this time?
• What part of your physical life could do with a boost?
• What kind of future are you willing to work toward?

Keywords
Financial opportunity, a physical boost, a bonus

Reversed: *Wasted opportunity, lack of financial or business vision, feeling under the weather*

2 of Pentacles

In modern life, it is unusual to have just one responsibility at a time. It is more likely that we are expected to juggle different jobs, relationships, and roles simultaneously. The 2 of Pentacles is about maintaining all of these responsibilities and trying our best to dedicate enough time and energy to each.

Living out the role of the 2 of Pentacles can become a little like a juggling act. How do we find enough hours in the day to hold down a job, look after a family, eat healthily, and also take time to rest and recharge? Some people breeze through their daily tasks effortlessly, but the majority of us do not find it so easy. The busier life becomes, the more we are expected to carry.

While this card may feel like a burden and we might just be ready to voluntarily drop it all, it is worth remembering that the 2 of Pentacles is a card of coping. However we feel we are doing, we *are* managing to fulfill our responsibilities, and it is likely that those around us have confidence in our ability to do so.

2 of Pentacles as a Situation

The 2 of Pentacles will arise when our schedule is fuller than usual. We might feel as though we are running from one place to another, fulfilling as many commitments as humanly possible. Because the suit of Pentacles (or coins in some decks) is associated with finances, this card could also symbolize balancing accounts or moving money around so that everything and everyone is paid at the right time. It might not leave much for luxuries, though.

For some, the card will represent more than one job or career. The 2 of Pentacles might concern taking on extra work to make ends meet, or if we are starting a business, it may encourage us to run it alongside a day job until it has become established.

Within the world of love, multiple relationships could be indicated. For the single person, it could suggest the need to date more than one partner before making a decision about who to settle down with.

2 of Pentacles as a Person

As a person, we find a multitasker in this card; the person symbolized by the 2 of Pentacles seems to have everything under control. They might have their own business, a family, a full and fun social life, and still find the time to get the mundane chores of life completed. They might be the envy of others who are less able to juggle their own responsibilities.

In some situations, the 2 of Pentacles could represent a coping mechanism. If someone has been through a difficult period of time, keeping busy might be a natural way to work through their problems or even avoid them.

2 of Pentacles and You

- How well do you think you are coping at this point in time?
- What two areas of life do you think you juggle effectively?
- How might you find more balance in life?
- Would you consider yourself as being flexible and adaptable or resistant to change?

Keywords

Change, fluctuation, multitasking, balance, coping

Reversed: *Unable to cope, dividing your time between too many things, overwhelmed by responsibility*

3 of Pentacles

In the 3 of Pentacles, we become aware of our physical environment and the people around us. It's not always easy to function entirely by ourselves, and this card reminds us of how supportive a group of people can be.

Due to its connection to physical labor and work, the 3 of Pentacles will often speak about teamwork within our professional life. It reminds us that we might be just one cog among many. Of course, this doesn't undermine our importance, but it does remind us that a success is not ours alone. We all have individual skill sets and the 3 of Pentacles can regard an initial recognition of our own proficiency.

3 of Pentacles as a Situation

When the 3 of Pentacles shows its face in a reading, it suggests that working with others is vital to success. This could be imperative in either our professional or personal life. If you consider a stage performer for a moment, their art can only become truly realized with the help of those who have a professional understanding of lighting, sound, and set design. There are many people behind the scenes working toward the same goal, even if unseen. Every small cog in the greater machine of the performance is important for a goal to be realized.

In modern life, not everybody works with others. These days, there are many people who work from home or are self-employed. While there will still be other people to consult, the 3 of Pentacles could describe the different roles one must take on within their own business—the promoter, the web designer, the bookkeeper, and the gopher. The card could be asking us to disperse our energy among these different responsibilities. For all involved, initial success is indicated.

3 of Pentacles as a Person

As a person, the 3 of Pentacles could be considered as a team player. This is the kind of person who doesn't mind sharing in the work of the others and is happy to work with them.

The person described by the 3 of Pentacles understands that a specific goal can be accomplished only when everyone pulls together. They know that their part of the bigger picture is crucial, but no more important than anyone else's who is involved. In this sense, the card can be an awakening for an egotist. There will always be someone who feels that they are bigger than the group, and this may be the case when the 3 of Pentacles is in a challenging position. Self-importance and an inflated opinion of oneself will only hinder progress.

3 of Pentacles and You

• How many groups are you actively part of and what is your role in each?
• How well do you think you work as a team?
• How different does it feel to win as part of a team, rather than individually?
• Can you think of those people who help you achieve a task, whom might go unnoticed in the greater scheme of things?

Keywords

Teamwork, collaborating with others, not taking all the glory, initial accomplishment of a project

Reversed: *Bad team player, egotist, sloppy workmanship*

4 of Pentacles

The 4 of Pentacles helps us to manage our resources. Because the suit of Pentacles is connected to our physical life, this card will concern the control and organization of those things that are tangible—our money, security, and possessions.

As with many cards in the tarot, it is always important to find balance. The 4 of Pentacles can suggest that our need to control could be consuming us. In terms of our finances, we may be holding on to the things we have too tightly for fear of losing them. Of course, in some situations, this may be wise, but as a general rule of thumb, being unable to share assets can appear greedy or result in the drying up of our investments. Sometimes, we need to reinvest to maintain a flow, and spending a little money can actually encourage greater financial growth further down the line.

Even though the 4 of Pentacles might advise us to relinquish control to some extent, it primarily suggests sensible management of our assets. At its core, the card asks us to find balance between sharing and saving. While reinvestment and enjoying the fruits of our labor is important, there will be times when holding back a little cash for a rainy day or an unexpected cost could be beneficial too.

4 of Pentacles as a Situation

As a situation, the 4 of Pentacles will manifest in a tarot reading when some kind of attention to balance is needed. This will likely regard monetary matters. If you have been spending a little too much lately, the card will suggest pulling back for a bit. Hoarding can be associated with this card, so now might be a time to look at how important material possessions are and whether they are really needed to be happy.

When the 4 of Pentacles arrives in a reading, it could be asking you to make a small sacrifice. Are you saving up for a wedding, vacation, or new home? We never know what is around the corner, and this card suggests that tightening the proverbial belt could be beneficial in the long run for when an unexpected cost occurs.

4 of Pentacles as a Person

Traditionally, the 4 of Pentacles is often nicknamed the "card of the miser." It can depict someone who is frugal to the extreme. They may feel as though they are simply counting pennies but, to others, they could appear stingy.

In its most positive light, the 4 of Pentacles describes someone who is careful. They know what they have because they keep an eye on every detail. As a professional bookkeeper or accountant, such a close control over spending may be admirable, but under a personal lens, they could come across as being overly cautious or even tightfisted.

When the 4 of Pentacles depicts a romantic partner, it comes with a word of warning. Someone described by this card may view a partner in the same way as they view their property and might become possessive of what they consider to be theirs. As well as being reluctant to share their own time and money, this person may try to control their significant other's schedule, relationships, and individuality. Their love and affection could become stifling and one might end up feeling like just another of their possessions.

4 of Pentacles and You

• What or whom are you holding on to too tightly, through fear of loss?
• What situation or relationship are you trying to control at this time?
• Could you be a little less relaxed with your finances?
• Is there something you need to save for?

Keywords

Financial power, fear of change, money management, possessiveness

Reversed: *Miser, inflexibility, fear of loss, financial carelessness*

5 of Pentacles

Bumps in the road are inevitable, and the 5 of Pentacles reflects this. Due to the nature of Pentacles, it is likely that it is our physical resources that will take a hit.

The 5 of Pentacles is a card of physical loss and, most often, it is concerned with poverty and lack. This will likely concern money, but some readers also link the card to poor health and a lack of physical well-being.

The 5 of Pentacles may appear bleak, but each of the difficult cards in the tarot deck offers lessons. In difficult times, we learn about whom we can depend upon and which friends are willing to help us when the chips are down.

5 of Pentacles as a Situation

Most of us can recall a time when we've hit a financial slump or have felt bogged down by the world around us. The 5 of Pentacles needn't be a financial catastrophe, though; more likely, it will represent those times when we find it difficult to make ends meet. The card could arise to indicate the end of the financial month, when money is tight, or act as a reminder to be more frugal.

Often, the 5 of Pentacles can speak about how we feel during periods of lack. Many of us will lose faith in the future and wonder how we'll make it through lean times. This can lead to feelings of isolation and a fear of reaching out for help.

5 of Pentacles as a Person

As a person, the 5 of Pentacles describes somebody who is down on their luck. In some readings, this will act as a one-off description, highlighting someone who is presently suffering financial or physical hardship. When this card shows up frequently, however, it defines someone who is consistently having trouble with finances or is experiencing chronic health problems.

In challenging positions, the 5 of Pentacles can describe someone who doesn't want to help themselves. They may have become used to a difficult way of life and have lost any hope of things changing. Unhealthy lifestyles or bad money management could be indicated, but at this time, this person is either unable or unwilling to take responsibility for their part in the downfall.

5 of Pentacles and You

• Can you remember a time of physical or financial hardship in your past? If so, how did you manage to move on from it?
• How might you prepare yourself for leaner financial times?
• How does lack affect your self-confidence?
• If you are currently going through a difficult patch, what prevents you from losing faith in the future?

Keywords

Loss, financial lack, health issues, feeling isolated

Reversed: *Renewed faith, financial recovery, unjustified financial worry*

6 of Pentacles

The 6 of Pentacles is a card of physical balance. While it can be favorable in financial situations, it is not a card of abundance. Instead, it suggests assistance showing up when it is required.

At best, the 6 of Pentacles regards support. When it enters a reading, the card might highlight help from a person or organization, or it could indicate a financial boost just when you need it. This card, in essence, restores balance. Many readers will suggest that financial harmony will be recovered or help is on its way, but for balance to really work, we must show our gratitude by "paying it forward." To pay it forward is to be generous with what we have. If you are going through a financial rut, you may wonder what you have left to give, but the 6 of Pentacles reminds us of the many charitable acts we can perform that cost time and energy rather than money.

6 of Pentacles as a Situation

The 6 of Pentacles can describe financial assistance of all kinds. It may turn up in a reading as a scholarship, a tax rebate, or a little financial aid. Although the suit of Pentacles will often relate to money, this card can concern more than financial injections. People's time is also a commodity, and the 6 of Pentacles could manifest as financial advice or even the ear of a friend when you're feeling down. Traditionally, the card is a symbol of charity, and whether you are the supporter or the supported could come down to your perception of a situation.

In a relationship reading, the 6 of Pentacles could depict an imbalance. Are you being supported by a partner, financially or otherwise? Or do you feel as though he or she is taking advantage of your goodwill?

6 of Pentacles as a Person

The person described by the 6 of Pentacles is a philanthropist. At best, this is someone who will step in and support us when we need it. Whether this is an anonymous donor or just someone who passes on secondhand baby clothes, a generous soul is indicated by this card. Selflessness is associated with this person, so the 6 of Pentacles will describe charity workers, volunteers, or anyone who puts their needs below the requirements of others. In a professional setting, however, this person could work within an area of financial aid or support services.

In the most challenging of positions, the 6 of Pentacles will describe someone who takes more than they give. For the highest good, this card concerns balance and a flow of resources, but there will always be someone who is comfortable to consistently receive and to give nothing in return.

6 of Pentacles and You

• Can you think of a relationship in your life that is unbalanced?
• Where might you find much-needed support at this time?
• What could you share or donate that you no longer need?
• What charity do you receive?

Keywords

Support, financial assistance, charity, generosity

Reversed: *One-sided generosity, resisting help, selfishness*

7 of Pentacles

The 7 of Pentacles is a card of harvest. When we have invested in a job, vocation, or relationship, this card will advise us to sit back and wait for the fruits of our labor. Things will take shape, but as with anything worthwhile, manifestation takes its own good time.

At its core, the 7 of Pentacles is a positive card. It reminds us that we've already put in a great deal of effort and will eventually be able to reap the rewards. For some of us, this will be frustrating news. Many of us live in a world of instant gratification and no longer need to be as patient as was once expected.

7 of Pentacles as a Situation

While not everything takes as long as it once did, there are always some processes that cannot be rushed—the birth of a baby, like the change of the seasons, is determined by nature. Similarly, we must wait for things like a piece of work to be published, exam results, or our business to become established. The 7 of Pentacles heralds a time of much-needed patience. Take a moment to evaluate where you are and what it has taken for you to get there. Things may be taking their time, but they are growing, even if it sometimes feels to the contrary.

Of course, this card does not encourage us to sit around and do nothing. While we wait for something to manifest in the physical world, the 7 of Pentacles gives us a little extra time to play with. When there is nothing more that can be done within a specific process, could we not invest our interest and enthusiasm into something else for the time being?

7 of Pentacles as a Person

The 7 of Pentacles describes someone who is patient but also persistent. This is the person who invests in something or someone, knowing that their investment will eventually pay off. In this sense, it suggests a person with foresight and faith. They are able to see the results before they have materialized and, in business, will have a feel for what could be a good deal.

At worst, the person described by the 7 of Pentacles is someone who frequently considers giving up. In a challenging position, this person is impatient and is likely to quit a project, relationship, or job if they do not see concrete results early on. There may be good reason to pull out of an investment, but this card could be reminding us that the best is yet to come, if we only remain patient long enough to see it materialize.

7 of Pentacles and You

• Would you describe yourself as patient or impatient?
• What have you invested in that you have not seen results from yet?
• Can you think of a process in your life that cannot be rushed?
• Why is patience considered a virtue?

Keywords

Patience, persistence, evaluation, assessment, slow but steady results

Reversed: *Rushed job, quitting too early, frustration, instant gratification*

8 of Pentacles

The 8 of Pentacles is a card of skill. Whether we are learning to read the tarot cards, drive a car, or build our own business, most people are in agreement that if we want to get as near to perfection as possible, we must practice.

In tarot tradition, the 8 of Pentacles is often referred to as the "card of the apprentice." An apprentice is someone who learns a craft from the bottom up, but there is no limit to the age of the student; we learn and develop new skills throughout our life, however old we are.

The 8 of Pentacles suggests a need for persistent effort and a willingness to perfect our practice. The more we work at something, the better we become at it.

8 of Pentacles as a Situation

The 8 of Pentacles might arrive in a reading to depict a new course of study. While its roots could lie within physical labor and creativity, it could easily concern learning the ropes of something like accountancy or bookkeeping skills. In fact, there is no limit as to what can be learned when this card is in play, should our motivation and interest become aroused.

Although the 8 of Pentacles could indicate a second career and the learning of a whole new discipline, it will probably turn up as something less dramatic. A promotion or a work-funded course are two examples of how this card's energy might manifest. Both will require training and development that will build on existing knowledge.

In a romantic reading, the 8 of Pentacles might advise us to put more effort into a relationship. The card reminds us to not become complacent. How might you work at becoming a better partner?

8 of Pentacles as a Person

The person described by the 8 of Pentacles is open to developing new skills. Within work, they could well be starting an apprenticeship or may already be involved within studies or training that will help them move up in their career.

As a personality, this person is not averse to starting at the bottom. They are both disciplined and persistent in their attainment of knowledge and practical understanding. The person described by the 8 of Pentacles will, however, display these characteristics in their personal life too. This is someone who is self-sufficient, wanting to know how things work and how to solve a problem for themselves rather than rely on anyone else. While it might not come easily to them at first, they are happy to invest their time and energy into practicing those things they know little about.

8 of Pentacles and You

• Are you interested in learning a new skill at this time?
• What have you mastered that took a lot of time and practice?
• What is your personal skill?
• What skills are you neglecting?

Keywords

Apprenticeship, hard worker, practice, skill, training

Reversed: *Laziness, shoddy workmanship, uncommitted, slapdash work*

9 of Pentacles

Within life, there are ample opportunities for us to draw on the support of others, but the 9 of Pentacles represents those accomplishments we have earned through the investment of our own blood, sweat, and tears.

Independence is the essence of the 9 of Pentacles. Despite the odds, it suggests the ability to succeed on our own merit. When this card comes into play, it acknowledges personal achievements, material gain, and enough business acumen to work independently. Traditionally, strong women have identified with this card in their readings, but the energy of this card will be relatable to anyone who has carved out their own place in the world or who has a comfortable life of their own making.

9 of Pentacles as a Situation

The 9 of Pentacles is considered fortunate within a reading, but this is far from being a card of random luck. When found in the present position, it provides a definite nod to a commitment that has already been made. If it rests in the future, then the card suggests that we can achieve the lifestyle we dream of only if we devote time and effort to it. Usually, it takes practice and accepting the odd setback to get to this level of success, but the 9 of Pentacles, when in the future, suggests we have what it takes to overcome the pitfalls that prevent others from succeeding.

The 9 of Pentacles could indicate self-employment within a reading, but it will represent any situation where self-sufficiency has paid off. When we draw this card, we can feel satisfied with where we are in life, since the card is often connected to personal wealth and luxurious surroundings.

9 of Pentacles as a Person

As a person, the 9 of Pentacles can describe someone with fortitude and strength of character. Although it's not always the case, we accept that a level of success or a grand lifestyle is something a person has worked up to through time and commitment. There is a feeling of security and well-deserved accomplishment in the person described by this card. They will likely own property, run their own business, or be a recognized figure of wealth in their community.

While the card obviously promises the fruits of individual labor, it is important to remember that all of the 9s in tarot (relating to The Hermit) have a solitary edge to them. As we have heard many times, it can be lonely at the top. Although there is comfort and luxury in the 9 of Pentacles, the card can depict someone who is set aside from others and feels as though they need to protect their assets. The love of the good life could prevent them from identifying with other people or developing a meaningful relationship.

9 of Pentacles and You

• How self-sufficient are you?
• What luxuries and comfort have you earned and can be proud of?
• Can you think of a strong and independent person, such as the one suggested by the 9 of Pentacles?
• What do you think the downfalls of success and luxury might be?

Keywords

Personal success, self-sufficiency, independence, luxury

Reversed: *Financial difficulties, dependency on others, loneliness*

10 of Pentacles

At its heart, the 10 of Pentacles is a card of comfort, wealth, and security. This is not, however, the luxurious personal wealth of the 9 of Pentacles. Instead, it is the stability of family or community that we are privileged to share and receive.

The 10 of Pentacles is a fortuitous card, since its riches needn't always be earned. In tradition, this card is connected to the wealth of family members, ancestors, and, in some cases, can highlight security through inheritance. Anyone seeking confirmation of an investment paying out or financial contentment in the future will be pleased to see this card in their reading. If the card sits within their past, then it could suggest that family money or the assistance of an organization has played a big part in the comfort they are currently experiencing.

10 of Pentacles as a Situation

While the 10 of Pentacles is an obvious symbol of wealth and financial assets, it doesn't necessarily mean that you are set to receive a monetary windfall or will soon be living a life of luxury. Security means something different to all of us, and in its most broad sense, it hints at a life without worry. When this card falls within a reading, it could be asking us to think about what is needed for us to feel secure within our daily life or how comfortable we already are.

The 10 of Pentacles has been traditionally linked to the family unit and the support of loved ones. As a situation, it could be asking us to think about the foundations of our own family and how we intend to help support them. Rather than this card always being about what we inherit or receive from others, it might be asking what we have to pass down. Money and property could be part of this, but time, wisdom, and experience are assets that mustn't be overlooked.

10 of Pentacles as a Person

The person described by the 10 of Pentacles will feel safe within their own skin. It is likely that they will be in both good health and good wealth, feel supported, and be comfortable.

Due to the inherent wealth associated with this card, the person described by the 10 of Pentacles could be living off of the wealth of someone else. The card might manifest as a rich kid who drives around in a car their parents bought them, or maybe it refers to someone who has received a more-than-generous divorce settlement from their ex. The foundations of their comfort will often stem from blood or close community ties, rather than being built up through their own hard work and diligence.

10 of Pentacles and You

• What would it take to make you feel secure?
• How much money do you really need?
• What do you have that you can hand down to others?
• How does the 10 of Pentacles relate to your own family?

Keywords

Stability, foundation, financial security, inheritance, family ties

Reversed: *Problems with security, financial problems, poor investments, debt*

Page of Pentacles

The Page of Pentacles is connected with the element of Earth, so he or she is often associated with those things that are tangible. Pentacles are usually concerned with finances, but this youth might be interested in outdoor pursuits or involved in physical labor.

Page of Pentacles as a Person

The Pentacles Court are the laborers of the tarot, and the Page of Pentacles is no exception. As with all of the Pages, they are a student learning the ropes of their element. In this card, we find someone who is committed to the job at hand. Because this suit leans toward the physical, this young person could be a junior craftsperson, an apprentice, or someone developing a manual skill. We might also find them working in sports and leisure, since they are concerned with physical health and enjoy keeping active.

The Page of Pentacles has learned to take care of their money. They might not have a lot of it, but at best, they are careful with their finances. In their professional life, they might be found working in a financial institution, as a trainee accountant, or in a job where they handle money. When this card is in a challenging position, finances might become an issue, since they could be spending more than they save or earn.

Page of Pentacles as a Situation

As a bearer of news, the Page of Pentacles can represent messages regarding money. When positively dignified, they might represent a check in the mail, a tax rebate, or even news of a small cash win. Messages brought by this Page will likely be delivered by hand.

When the Page of Pentacles enters a reading, they suggest new beginnings of a physical nature. Since they work so hard, they might present an opportunity to invest in something from the bottom—whether through hard work or cash investment—and build a foundation for the future. Out of all the Pages, the Page of Pentacles is the most sensible. If the card represents someone entering your life, then it is probable that they will be dependable and committed.

Page of Pentacles and You
• What practical skills would be worth learning at this time?
• Are you good with money, like this Page, or does it slip through your fingers?
• What might you invest in right now, whether financially or through effort?
• Can you think of someone whose diligence and committed attitude reminds you of this Page?

Keywords
Practical, apprentice, sporty, financial planning, foresight, student

Reversed: *Spendthrift, idle, time-wasting, bad financial investment*

Knight of Pentacles

The Knight of Pentacles is grounded within the element of Earth and is, therefore, concerned with the practical and tangible aspects of daily life.

Knight of Pentacles as a Person

Of all the four Knights, the Knight of Pentacles moves the slowest. This is because he (though the knight can also represent a female) is careful and considered in his actions, and he doesn't rush a job. He knows that it takes time and effort to do something properly, and he doesn't intend to cut corners. Due to his physical commitment, he is both respected and dependable.

In a relationship, the Knight of Pentacles is loyal and trustworthy. He might not be as charismatic as some of the other Knights, but he makes up for that by being attentive, punctual, and having staying power. As a lover or prospective partner, he mightn't be as dynamic as his tarot cousins, but he has the ability to last the distance where they may flounder.

It is important to remember that this young man is also connected to money and finance. Due to his careful nature, the Knight of Pentacles is the saver who is eager to put a little aside or invest in the future.

In a challenging position, this card can highlight an individual who places too much importance on the material things in life. Sometimes it describes a person who is idle, and who might let money slip through his fingers. He might even be described as being frugal with his cash when flanked by difficult cards in a reading.

Knight of Pentacles as a Situation

The Knight of Pentacles can be a good omen when viewed as a situation. Due to his slow movement, he might not speak of an overnight success, but we can be assured that whatever we're waiting for will make good in the end. With this in mind, business deals or potential relationships can be viewed as sound and are worth investing in. Profit, whether in love or business, will be rewarded through taking part in the long game.

Travel accompanies all of the four Knights, and with the Knight of Pentacles we encounter slow and steady journeys. Of course, this will include journeying by foot. Because he relates to both money and work, he could symbolize traveling for business or even big shopping trips.

Knight of Pentacles and You

- Can you think of someone like the Knight of Pentacles, who is not afraid to roll up his sleeves and get on with the job?
- What might you need to invest your effort and commitment into at this time?
- How would you describe your relationship with the material things in life?
- Are you a saver or a spender?

Keywords

Trustworthy, dependable, hard worker, committed, slow progress

Reversed: *Lazy, materialistic, spendthrift, shallow*

Queen of Pentacles

The Queen of Pentacles is connected to her physical environment. Being a practical and efficient member of her family and the community, she prefers a hands-on approach to a situation and understands the value of her physical resources.

Queen of Pentacles as a Person

As a nurturer of the earth, this Queen may be found in nature. Her connection to the physical world might link her to her garden, an outdoor job, or subjects of an environmental nature. But while she could symbolize a keen gardener or environmentalist, it's important to note that she treats all living things with the same kindness and respect. The Queen of Pentacles is often portrayed as the Earth Mother, but on a day-to-day basis, this may describe someone who dotes on their children and is heavily involved in their upbringing.

Of all four Queens, the Queen of Pentacles is the most pragmatic. While her tarot sisters may overthink a problem or let it affect them emotionally, this lady will break down an obstacle into manageable pieces and deal with it in the simplest way possible. Whether this concerns removing a thorn from her pet's paw, deciding on the best way to get the car loaded up, or figuring out how to get a lost ball down from a tree, this woman assesses the situation quickly and gets to work in the most practical way she can.

The suit of Pentacles is associated with money, so this lady is at home with her finances. She has a head for figures and knows how to stretch her resources. She may be the envy of her friends, since she always seems to find a bargain, and if she can't find what she's after, she will take a stab at creating it herself. In her career, she could be linked to finances and money management—possibly as an accountant or a financial advisor. She is committed and forward thinking, knowing that it takes time and effort to get where one wants to be. Due to her determination, you'll find her in the more powerful positions of her industry.

When this Court character becomes challenging in a reading, she can take on quite a different persona. This is the person who puts material wealth before the welfare of others and may be quick to show off what she's got. Whether she spends what she has or goes into debt for it, she must have the latest fashions and accessories.

Queen of Pentacles as a Situation

The Queen of Pentacles, as a situation, might be asking us to assess and work out our finances. Is more money going out than coming in? This card advises that we go through our accounts with a fine-tooth comb and look for ways in which we can manage money more efficiently. If you don't have a head for figures, it might be time to employ an accountant or ask a friend to give the books a once-over.

The Queen of Pentacles is a natural caregiver. While she might be speaking of our own maternal instincts, she could be advising that we take greater care of ourselves. When we are working or playing too hard, we can forget to look after our bodies, which can result in poor health. When this Queen appears as a situational card, she may be asking us to consider a change in diet, routine, or lifestyle—one which would greater benefit our well-being. Spending time in the sunshine or getting some exercise might be key to restoring balance.

Queen of Pentacles and You

- Can you think of someone like the Queen of Pentacles, who is practical and naturally efficient?
- Are you overly careful with your financial resources, or not careful enough?
- How connected to nature and your physical environment are you?
- How important are material possessions to you?

Keywords

Practical, responsible, caring, business-savvy, nature-loving, good with finances

Reversed: *Bad with finances, a show-off, irresponsible, greedy, lazy*

King of Pentacles

The King of Pentacles is a master of physical security. Grounded within a foundation of hard work, he is a respected individual, often connected with the physical world in all of its manifestations.

King of Pentacles as a Person

The suit of Pentacles is often concerned with finances, and this is an area that the King is very comfortable with. Having worked hard to earn his money, he is now in a position of stability, where he can advise others from his own experience. As a professional, this man may work as a financial advisor, property expert, or business investor. He knows how to make money and uses his know-how to teach others to do the same. Not every King of Pentacles will be a professional advisor or big-time investor, though. He might simply appear in a reading to signify someone who is shrewd and careful with his cash.

The suit of Pentacles is ruled by the element of Earth. While this King is likely to be in a place of personal security, he needn't always be associated with finances. He can be found working out in nature, with the sun on his back, or within some kind of managerial role related to construction work.

The King of Pentacles is a generous man, and despite his need to meticulously account for his finances, he is happy to support those whom he believes deserve his assistance. If he can get a return on his investment, then even better. When he is in a challenging position, this man may try to buy the affections of others, flash his cash, or, at worst, become miserly and even greedy.

King of Pentacles as a Situation

The King of Pentacles could be asking us to be mature with our money. While investment is a possibility, the card advises that we take greater care of our finances and pay more attention to what is coming in and going out. You may not own a fortune, but this king suggests that we take care of what we do have.

There are times when we need to seek professional advice around money, property, and investment, and this card could be encouraging us to do that (rather than take a chance alone). The King of Pentacles can act in this role to provide you with sound advice. He might be an accountant or a local bank manager. If you are having trouble with money, he might even represent someone who could provide a loan. When in a challenging position, however, this King could describe the assistance of an untrustworthy and unprofessional loan shark, who has no intention of doing you any favors.

King of Pentacles and You

- How capable are you of dealing with your finances?
- Do you need to be shrewd with your money?
- Who might you go to if you need some sound financial or business advice?
- Can you think of someone who likes to show off how much money they have to make themselves look good?

Keywords

Security, stability, financial advice, trustworthy, disciplined

Reversed: *materialistic, dominant, dishonest, financially undisciplined*

4

BECOMING ADEPT & SPREADS

Learning to Read the Tarot

Regardless of what you may have heard, tarot reading is not something that can be learned overnight. Even if you manage to memorize the seventy-eight meanings with ease, it takes time to absorb what each card means to you on a personal level. This can be said of any art. A dancer might have rhythm, but they must marry this natural ability with time and discipline if they wish to excel. As with anything, the best results come with consistent effort.

Before we view a few useful and well-known spreads, let's look at some of the most frequently asked questions about learning to read the tarot cards.

How Long Will It Take for Me to Learn to Read?

This is a difficult question to answer because learning is different for everyone, and your reading ability might depend on how much time you have to invest in practicing.

Learning the tarot is a journey. Any professional tarot reader will tell you that there are no shortcuts when it comes to learning to read. However, with every reading, reflection, or tidbit of learned information, the cards will reveal a bit more about themselves, and this is the fun and magical part of dedicating your time to this art. When most new students realize that learning the tarot is a process, rather than a goal to be reached, they relax and enjoy the experience far more.

Tarot is a language: a language of symbols. Would you be able to read a French phrasebook in one evening, then pop over to France the next day and speak French fluently, understanding all its dialects and colloquialisms? Of course you couldn't, and it is the same with tarot. The most important thing you must remember is to not beat yourself up about the length of time it takes to become familiar with the cards. Most of us do not "get it" right away, and being patient is a far more effective method of approach than pressuring yourself to learn as quickly as possible. With French as an example, once people have immersed themselves in it and have begun to use their new skills with others, they soon become more competent, even if there are times when they encounter a word or phrase with which they are less familiar. Take your time: there is no rush.

There will never be a point where you know all there is to know about the tarot—to do so would be akin with knowing all there is to know about life—but, with consistent practice, you will eventually feel comfortable with your cards.

How Often Should I Use the Tarot?

When beginning to learn, I would advise that you use the cards every day. This might sound like a tall order, but it needn't be a chore.

Learning the tarot could be likened to exercise. You might buy yourself a new gym outfit, tell everyone you're going to get fit, and for that first week, you work out every day. While you might be exercising every night of the week for the first fortnight, something invariably comes up that causes you to miss a session. From then on, you miss another one and another until your gym visits eventually grind to a halt.

People have busy lives, filled with work, family, and relationships, so you might wonder how you can fit tarot reading into your daily routine. When we push ourselves too hard, we end up losing interest, so I would recommend beginning your practice gently. Even if you want to invest every waking moment in your new hobby, reading one card a day is acknowledged as a great way to start off. It is important that you pull this card at a time when you know you have ten minutes to spare—not as you're dashing out the door or while you are in the middle of something else.

A card drawn in the morning can be used for guidance during your day. You might want to stand it up where you can see it or even carry it with you. You may become aware of things that relate to the card's message or even problems that it might answer. Alternatively, drawing a card before bed, when you are relaxed and reflective, can allow for you to casually think over your day and consider how the card's meaning is relevant. The more often that you do this, the easier it will become for you to build up a routine. You needn't spend an hour with the card (unless you want to), but allowing ten minutes to absorb what it means for you can be valuable in building up your knowledge and understanding.

New and even experienced readers alike keep a log of their card draws and discoveries. You may want to jot the card name and a few sentences into an exercise book, a diary, or on a calendar. Keeping a record allows you to see the patterns that emerge in your card draws, so that you can look back at how they have mirrored or influenced your path. Understanding tarot on a personal level is imperative to developing your bond with the deck. Once you can recognize your own experiences within the cards, you'll have a better chance of explaining them to other people.

When Should I Start Reading with Spreads?

One of the biggest mistakes a new reader makes is to jump straight into the larger spreads. This is not always their fault, since the pamphlets that come with many decks do not include shorter spreads or much information about how to use them. What happens, more often than not, is that the larger spreads leave a new reader confused, and they end up becoming frustrated and soon give up.

While I have included the traditional Celtic Cross spread in this book (which carries ten cards), I would not suggest you tackle it until you have a good understanding of the seventy-eight tarot cards and can confidently handle smaller spreads. My advice to anyone starting out is to keep things simple. There is so much information that can be gleaned from a three-card draw or even from pulling just one card. There will be plenty of time to try out the larger spreads further down the line, but to begin with, I believe that it is better to read three cards well than ten cards badly.

Not all readers use spreads. While it can be liberating to read the cards without a structure, it can also become confusing. Using a spread that has defined positions for the cards we draw highlights our intention from the start. If a card falls in the position of the past, then we are already halfway to formulating an interpretation. We will know that the card symbolizes something or someone that has passed out of our lives or who is still impacting on a situation, though no longer around.

How Do I Begin a Reading?

How one approaches a reading is individual to each reader. There are, however, a few things I would advise before starting.

Taking a few moments to prepare for a reading is essential. Regardless of where you are, a few minutes spent in quiet contemplation is a good start. You may wish to hold your tarot deck and ask your spiritual guides, ancestors, or the universe for a little assistance with your work. Whether this is something you say out loud, like a prayer in an opening ceremony, or in your mind, it is your intention that is important. An affirmation of some kind could be spontaneous or something you recite each time. When I prepare for a reading, I ask that I might receive guidance for the benefit of all involved.

Not everybody uses a question or subject for a reading, but it can be a very useful technique. Without one, you might be left wondering if the cards are

talking about one's love life or
career. Posing a question such
as "How might I move forward
most efficiently in my work life?"
gives the reading some body
and a frame to work within. The
question you or the subject of
your reading asks will need a
little consideration and thought,
because a poorly formed question
will result in a vague answer.
I have found that questions
requiring a yes or no answer

rarely work. Instead, it is important that you ask a question that places the
power in the hands of the person being read for. For example, think about the
difference between "Will I find a boyfriend this year?" and "What might I do to
support my search for a romantic relationship?"

I am often asked how to set up a reading table. To perform a good reading,
the only real essential is a set of tarot cards, but many readers do like to
decorate their reading space. This is a matter of personal taste. You might wish
to place a few favorite crystals around your setting, light some incense sticks,
or lay out a pretty cloth to read upon. While none of these are a necessity, they
can help a reader get into the mood and add a little magic to the experience.

How Soon Can I Read for Others?

There is nothing worse than getting a reading from someone who continually
consults their tarot manual, so I suggest that you become familiar with the
seventy-eight cards before you read for someone else. Once you have an idea of
what each means, reading for others can be a great way of gaining experience
and practice. It can become tedious to solely read about your own issues, so
successfully charting someone else's life through the cards can be rewarding.

When you begin to read for others, it is important that you state you are
still learning. Friends and relatives will be only too pleased to play guinea pig,
but we must remember that the situations and issues within their cards must
still be handled with care. Letting others know that you are still an apprentice

is mutually beneficial, since it will reduce the amount of responsibility you have to cope with, and it will allow a little room for the odd mistake here and there.

There will be some who do not wish to read for others, and that is their choice, but reading for other people allows for a greater scope of subject matter than only delving into your own situations and answering your own personal questions can provide. Though not impossible, it can be difficult to read our own cards, since we naturally have our own hopes and fears about what a card might mean. Reading for someone we know less well allows the card to speak its truth, without being tarnished by wishful thinking or apprehension.

Should I Use More Than One Deck?

As mentioned at the beginning of this book, there are currently thousands of decks on the market. Exploring the archetypes across tarot sets can be a rewarding and enjoyable experience, seeing how each creator has chosen to represent their cards. As a collector of tarot decks, I have hundreds of sets, which I have gathered over my twenty years of study. Tarot can be addictive, and it is easy to become swept away by new titles and fads, hoping that the next deck will provide you with something that the last didn't.

When beginning, though, I would advise sticking with a pack that you resonate with until you understand its basic structure, intention, and meanings. From my own experience, switching between decks can really inhibit growth and learning and become confusing. Knowing what I do now, I'd have started with a standard deck and used it until I was proficient, as switching between different packs and systems certainly held me back. This is why a little research before buying a deck is beneficial. If you have the opportunity to find out about a deck, or even try it out before purchasing, you will get a better idea about what will work for you. The internet is a good starting point when searching for a deck. I advise using the same set at least until you are comfortable enough to read without the book. When you have a working knowledge of the seventy-eight cards, you might want to expand your collection.

Spreads

The One-Card Spread

Pulling just one card can be
underrated. Those who are new
to tarot reading often assume that
drawing more cards will result in a
better reading. This is not necessarily
true. Using just one card allows us to
focus our intent on just one question
and answer. For example, if we wish
to know how we can improve our
lifestyle and receive The Fool in a
single-card draw, there is little doubt
that the card suggests we take a
chance and try something new. If we
ask who can help us with a specific
problem and draw The Emperor,
we'd do well to seek the assistance of
someone who is well-organized and
experienced. This may not reflect all
areas of our life in one hit, but it can
pinpoint what we need to concentrate on first.

A one-card reading is perfect for a beginner because of its immediacy. You
simply ask a question, shuffle your cards, and pull one. Once drawn, let your
intuition do the work. What are your first feelings about the card? Try not
to allow fear or fantasy to cloud your vision, but instead listen to what your
intuition advises.

Just-Before-Bed Spread

Many readers pull a card as guidance for the forthcoming day, and this spread is a variation of that practice. As its title suggests, this spread is most effective in the evening when you are feeling relaxed and reflective.

CARD 1

This card asks us to look back at our day and those things we have learned within it. Did someone impart words of wisdom? Maybe the card drawn will remind us of the support we received from a friend or colleague. Alternatively, it could signify how we are feeling about something that has happened.

CARD 2

The second card gives us an idea of what to expect tomorrow. Does the card reveal someone who will be important in the following day, or does it depict something that might manifest? For some, it could suggest an approach they may need to take. As an example, the 7 of Wands may remind us to stand up for our beliefs and not allow others to take advantage of us.

This spread is a good one for the beginner, since it encourages the use of a card for reflection, enabling us to layer up the tarot cards with our own personal experiences. It also allows a reader to use the cards as a way of assessing their usefulness ahead of a situation.

The Three-Card Spread

One of the most common layouts used in tarot is the humble three-card spread. What makes this spread a classic is its immense versatility. It is most often used to look at the past, present, and future of a specific situation:

CARD 1

This first card looks at the past and highlights those things that may be less important than present influences but still have some bearing on a situation. As an example, a previous carefree decision, pinpointed by The Fool, may have a profound effect on the present.

CARD 2

This card looks at the present time. This card describes what is important right now. A card such as The Magician would suggest that we are in a place of great personal power and have relevant resources to draw on.

CARD 3

The final card in this spread provides a projection of the future and gives insight into where we are headed. As an example, the 5 of Pentacles could detect a lack of money on the horizon. This is, however, a positive card to draw here because it encourages us to make changes before this time of hardship hits. Working out a budget or putting a little money aside could prevent the energy of this card from being harsher than necessary.

    The three positions in this spread can be adjusted to fit any subject, and this is why it is so popular. Rather than using the layout to delve into the

past, present, and future, you might want to change the positions to mind, body, and spirit or situation, obstacle, and advice. The possibilities are endless.

The Celtic Cross Spread

The Celtic Cross is one of the most famous spreads, and it can be found in most books about tarot. It is also the one spread that divides readers: many can see how versatile and effective the layout can be, whereas others find it to be complicated and too rigid. Personally, I like this spread a lot and use it for all of my professional readings.

The Celtic Cross takes a long time to perfect. While it is not the best choice for a beginner, it shouldn't be pushed aside entirely. If you try to jump into it straight away, it will only confuse you, but once you are comfortable with the cards and smaller layouts, this spread will make far more sense than it does on first glance.

What makes this a complicated spread is that the cards work best when they are read in relation to one another. As we look further into this spread, I will outline some of the combinations that I look for in a reading.

CARD 1—SITUATION

What situation are the cards addressing? A card in this position refers to what is happening and how we might be feeling in relation to it.

CARD 2—CHALLENGE

What crosses us at this time? This card will speak of blockages that challenge the situation. When a positive card sits here, we may wish to consider its reversed meaning or a way in which the essence of the card is blocked.

CARD 3—FOUNDATION AND THE UNCONSCIOUS MIND

This is the root of the reading and looks at the deeper issues at hand. It could describe influences that reach into our distant past or might simply speak about what the real root of the problem is. A positive card in this position will determine those things or people that give us strength, whereas a negative one could explain why a problem is continuing to recur. It also pertains to the unconscious mind, as it could highlight something we'd not realized was an issue, lying deeper within our own psyche.

The Celtic Cross Spread

Orientation

························

Whether you do this reading, or any other, the traditional way or with your own twist, it's easiest to lay the cards out so they face you, the reader, even if you are doing the reading for someone else. If you try to lay the cards out so they are upright from the subject of the reading's perspective, things can get confusing!

For in-person readings, I often ask people if they'd like to pop round my side of the table afterward to take a photograph, or I sometimes send "my view" to clients after a Skype reading for their reference. Of course, you can always sit on the same side of the table with the subject so that you are both viewing it from the same direction.

CARD 4—RECENT PAST

This position highlights recent events. In some cases, these people or energies will no longer be active, but there will be occasions where they might still have a residual impact, even if they are "out of sight."

CARD 5—YOUR FOCUS AND THE CONSCIOUS MIND

The top card of the cross suggests what we are focusing on. It explains our conscious thoughts about the situation. A positive card could describe a healthy mind-set, while a negative one may suggest we are being held back by fear or distrust.

CARD 6—NEAR FUTURE

A card in this position will advise where we are headed. This card looks at weeks, rather than a longer time frame, and gives an indication of what (or who) might arise on the not-so-distant horizon.

CARD 7—YOU

The "You" card is extremely important because it provides a glimpse into our motivations and how we are presenting ourselves at this time. All other cards in the spread will be colored by this card. If our future looks bright but we are feeling out of sorts or fearful, then achieving what we are truly capable of might be less obtainable than it needs to be. Alternatively, an overly confident attitude shown in this position could be termed as arrogance by others.

CARD 8—ENVIRONMENT

This card provides a glimpse of our personal environment and the people within it. If a Court card sits here, it will describe who is available for support or who could present a problem. Other cards may describe opportunities that are up for grabs or even the views of those involved in the situation.

CARD 9—HOPES AND FEARS

It might seem as though our hopes and fears are two different things, but you'd be surprised how the two are entwined. Often, our biggest dreams have the potential to be scary and overwhelming when manifested. Use your intuition when reading this position, because a card will highlight either a hope or a concern, but when we consider that it has the potential to be both, we can receive some interesting insight.

CARD 10—PROJECTED OUTCOME

In many descriptions of the Celtic Cross, commentators will title this card "Outcome." I have amended this because I do not believe that an outcome is set in stone. The card in this position shows a projection of where we *could* end up. This is where the real work in this spread begins, because we may need to adjust our behavior to either match or avoid the projection that the cards are hinting at.

How Can the Celtic Cross Spread Be Read Effectively?

Many people find the Celtic Cross overwhelming because there are so many cards. With this in mind, the spread can be broken up in a multitude of ways. In fact, if we look closely at the layout, we can see that there are actually many two- and three-card spreads within it. There are far too many to outline here, and part of the fun is in finding them yourself anyway. To get you started, though, I will outline some of the ones I look for:

The "You" Card

Personally, I find the "You" card (position 7) to be the most important card in the layout. It can be very telling about how we approach the world around us. It really doesn't matter what opportunities are available to us if the seventh card presents us as being apathetic and unwilling to see them. Alternatively, if we view the world with enthusiasm and an open mind (and the seventh card reflects this), we're more likely to make use of the things and people on offer.

Some readers use what is known as a *significator* in a reading, which is a card drawn to describe the person being read for. I find that the card in this position performs that role, highlighting the person's demeanor at the time. I will often turn this card first to gauge how the person is viewing the situation described and the greater world around them. It can be useful to describe this to a sitter, or reflect on it when reading for yourself, before turning the other cards over.

Though it might be time-consuming, it can be helpful to see how the seventh card reacts to every other card in the reading. Remember, the "You" card is not a representation of one's complete character; it simply acts as a mirror, showing how they are behaving at the time of a reading. A generally positive person may be going through a lull or recovering from a difficult time, and a card that is perceived as negative could reflect this in the present moment.

EXAMPLE 1

Let's say that we find the 8 of Swords in the seventh position. We might understand that this person is affected by constrictive thoughts and is feeling unable to see their way forward. The Emperor in the third position (Foundation) could well describe rules, an authority figure, or some kind of oppression that has caused them to lack self-confidence or the ability to think for themselves in the present.

EXAMPLE 2

If the Judgement card sits in the seventh position for someone who is looking for love, we can assume that they have decided to rethink their life, put the past behind them, and concentrate on a new relationship. If the Knight of Cups appears in position 4 (recent past), we might see the person whom was left behind. A Court in position 6 (near future), however, suggests a new romantic possibility or invitation. With a positive outlook, one is more likely to embrace this potential relationship and notice the new person's arrival.

Your Recent Past and Your Near Future

POSITIONS 4 AND 6

Cards 4 and 6 have an obvious relationship. At this point in time, we are standing directly between the two. We have an idea of where we have been and may have some idea of where we are headed. The card in position 6 (near future) may offer little surprise or it could throw a curveball. Whether we decide to catch it or stand aside and let it pass will be dependent on our current state of mind and our present hopes and fears.

EXAMPLE

Since many ask about love and romantic relationships, let's say that The Lovers sits in the recent past. This might concern a previous union or it may even remind us that a current partnership has seen better days.

In the near future, a card that is perceived as negative, such as the 10 of Swords, will be dependent on one's intuitive perception. It could mean that we are hanging on to a relationship that is not working, or it may suggest that we need to work through difficulties with our partner if we want our relationship to flourish again.

While the mutual respect and love of The Lovers has passed, it alerts us to its importance. We are being asked whether we want to persevere and get back on track, or if it is time to accept that things are over. It might not be an easy transition, but it probably is a necessary one that shouldn't be avoided any longer.

Your Focus, Hopes, and Fears

POSITIONS 5 AND 9

It is interesting to look at what we are focusing on during a reading. It is important to realize that what we are focusing on will not always be in our best interest. This is where the elements within the Minor Arcana can be helpful. If a reading concerns one's career, it might be detrimental for a card of emotion (Cups) to be in the fifth position. It might inform us that we need to be more practical and distance ourselves from our emotions within business.

If what we hope for is highlighted in position 9 (instead of the card showing what we fear), then it is often worth checking if our focus is in alignment with it. It could just take a small adjustment in our focus to get things on track.

EXAMPLE

If a personal wish (position 9) is signified by the 9 of Pentacles, it is likely that self-sufficiency is what's desired, because the 9 of Pentacles is a card of accomplishment and deserved success. If a card such as the 3 of Pentacles falls into focus, then it would suggest that we are on track for fulfilling our dreams. However, should a card like the 7 of Pentacles be found in position 5, the road forward might require greater patience or even a change of direction.

Try to Find Your Own Pairings

There are so many ways of pairing up cards within the Celtic Cross—far too many to list here. Here are a few more to get you started. Try them out and see which ones work for you.

- Is the conscious mind (card 5) in alignment with unconscious desires (card 3), or are they contrasting?
- How does the crossing card (card 2) inhibit the energy of the general atmosphere (card 1)?
- How does the near future (card 6) vary from the projected outcome (card 10)?
- What is the difference between our view of the world (card 7) and the opinions of those around us (card 8)?

INDEX